DYING TO LIVE

by
A.M. Hills

President of Texas Holiness University, Greenville, Texas

Author of

Backsliders and Worldly Christians
Cleansing Baptism
Establishing Grace
Fundamental Christian Theology
Homiletics and Pastoral Theology
Scriptural Holiness & Keswick Teaching Compared

$\mathbf{S}$

SCHMUL PUBLISHING COMPANY
NICHOLASVILLE, KENTUCKY

Published by Schmul Publishing Co.
PO Box 776
Nicholasville, KY 40340
USA

Printed in the United States of America

ISBN 10: 0-88019-604-1
ISBN 13: 978-0-88019-604-8

Visit us on the Internet at www.wesleyanbooks.com, or order direct from the publisher by calling 800-772-6657, or by writing to the above address.

Contents

DEDICATION

To those who are conscious of having lived unworthily and yet long for a larger and fuller life; and those who, in noble moments, aspire to usefulness, but somehow, amidst the mazes of a luxurious, worldly, self-seeking age, have missed their way and would be thankful for a friendly voice to lead them out, these pages are dedicated by their brother.

—THE AUTHOR

PUBLISHER'S PREFACE

Life! THAT IS THE MAIN THEME of A.M. Hills throughout this book. The author's ministry was wide, and his chief influence was as a scholar-evangelist in the holiness movement. At the time of publication of *Dying to Live* he was the president of Texas Holiness University near Greenville, Texas (later merged into what became known for many years as Bethany Nazarene College).

The book came about largely through the urging of W.B. Godbey, who heard Hills preach at the Revivalist camp at Cincinnati. He holds forth a wide view of the Christian life, but primarily he spotlights the need of heart holiness in order to truly live. He discusses the hopeless state of the unconverted, and shows the way to salvation through the blood of Jesus. With warnings against resisting the Holy Spirit, he holds up the great gift of entire sanctification, proclaiming that "death to self" is the prerequisite to victorious living.

It is a message that is still as viable in our day as it was in his.

—D. CURTIS HALE
Publisher, 2017

INTRODUCTION

THE SERMONS IN THIS VOLUME were prepared in the rush of my regular work, with no thought of publication. The last three sermons in this volume were preached at the Revivalist camp-meeting, near Cincinnati, O., in June, 1905, and taken down by shorthand reporters. After the preaching of the last one, dear old Dr. Godbey arose and put his arms around my neck, and said: "While you were preaching, God gave a message to me for you. He wants you to give a volume of sermons to the young preachers and teachers of Holiness, including the sermon you have preached this morning. I want you to grant me the privilege of writing the introduction." This is how I came to publish this book, and the following is the introduction written by Dr. Godbey:

AT 11 A.M., THE LAST SUNDAY of Salvation Park Camp-meeting, Ohio, 1905, Rev. A. M. Hills, D. D., President of the Texas Holiness University, preached a powerful sermon on the Holy Ghost, to a vast audience of Holiness people from all parts of the United States, British America, and quite a sprinkle from the Old World and the West India Islands. Seventy-five minutes they hung spellbound on the eloquent lips of the magnetic preacher;

his whole physiognomy, supernaturally radiant with the celestial splendor and flashing like lightning in all directions, was eminent from the indwelling Holy Ghost, whose glorious truth the man of God was heroically dispensing; he was even miraculously illuminated and energized by the Omnipotent Author.

The effects of the sermon on the multitude were marvelous. They seemed to be literally transported into the actual presence of the Almighty; overawed, electrified and thrillingly entranced, as if the archangel of doom had descended, and the dead were rising responsive to his trumpet call, and all gathering before the Great White Throne. In conclusion, responsive to the stentorian appeal of the enthusiastic preacher, "Will you be true to the Holy Ghost?" the entire multitude sprang to their feet, and scores made for the altar. A Pentecostal scene utterly indescribable followed; meanwhile, many prayed through into the kingdom, and pilgrims entered Beulah Land by dozens.

Meanwhile, God spoke to me to ask the preacher to publish the sermon, and with it as many others as He would give him, for the evangelization of the world, through the instrumentality of the Holiness people who are this day girdling the globe and preaching the Gospel of full salvation, pentecostal power, and the Lord's coming, to all nations. Therefore, this book is of Divine authorship, through the humble instrumentality of our excellent brother.

God is raising up an army of evangelists, male and female, in all nations, indiscriminate of race, color, nationality and religion; even miraculously saving and sanctifying the poor victims of sin, down at the bottom of slumdum; transforming saloon-keepers, drunkards, bums, thugs and harlots into flaming preachers of this glorious Gospel. A very small percentage of this vast evangelistic host, now preaching beneath every sky, has ever enjoyed educational opportunities. Therefore, it is really a *sine qua non* of their greatest possible efficiency to take all possible short cuts to the Biblical exegesis indispensable not only to qualify them to preach the everlasting Gospel, but to fortify them against the multitudinous, dangerous errors which Satan's counterfeit preachers are everywhere propagating to the fatal delusion and destruction of unsuspecting millions who are captured by their sophistries, hailing them as angels of light, while they are really wolves in sheep's clothing. Thus beguiled and hallucinated, they are led away till, hopelessly lassoed by Satan, they drop into Hell. Hence the transcendent importance on the part of all who preach the living Word, (*i.e.*, all of the Holiness people, who alone are competent to preach full salvation, from the simple fact that we can only efficiently preach what we experience), to fortify themselves by reading good books. Consequently, this book of sermons will prove a *thesaurus* of wisdom and guidance in the hands of our thousands of young preachers, who this day, washed in the blood and baptized with fire, are going to the ends of the earth. The Holiness books are, in God's providence, His teachers of His blessed Word. If you do not read them, you are in great danger of doing immense harm, and seriously damaging souls by preaching error. In this way the cause of Holiness has suffered much detriment. You may have a true and genuine experience and yet, through ignorance of the Bible, teach all sorts of error.

Now to the Father, Son and Holy Ghost, I commend this book of sermons, with all of the other valuable books written by its author, our beloved friend and brother in Christ. Showers of blessings on all who shall read this book.

—W.B. GODBEY

Sermon I
DYING TO LIVE
A Baccalaureate Sermon before the Graduating Class of Texas Holiness University, June 11, 1905.

John xii.23-28: "And Jesus answered them saying, The hour is come, that the Son of man should be glorified. Verily, verily, I say unto you, Except a grain of wheat fall into the earth and die, it abideth by itself alone; but if it die, it beareth much fruit. He that loveth his life loseth it, and he that hateth his life in this world shall keep it unto life eternal. If any man serve me, let him follow me; and where I am, there shall also my servant be: if any man serve me, him will the Father honour. Now is my soul troubled; and what shall I say? Father, save me from this hour. But for this cause came I unto this hour. Father, glorify thy name."

THIS PASSAGE IS ONE OF the most complete statements in the whole Word of God of the dignity and glory of self-sacrifice. The truth is here put with all the Savior's inimitable art of statement. Our thoughts are brought to consider the great law of sacrifice which, now dark and forbidding, and now radiant and glorious, runs through the whole creation of God. It is a law without which society could not hold together nor our race live; without which, indeed, the whole animal kingdom would become extinct. We shrink from sacrifice if we are base and selfish. We are drawn toward it if, and just so far as, we are noble. It is at once so difficult and so satisfying! so radically opposed to our innate selfishness, and so inseparably connected with our highest sympathies and noblest impulses! It is enshrined in our affections as connected with the life of Him who is the center of our faith. It is intimately interwoven with the highest theory and practice of Christian ethics. We must, therefore, in our religious study and meditations give this theme of sacrifice more than ordinary attention. We must study it; we must question it; we must wrestle with it until the gloom of its darkness changes into the radiance of its brighter aspects, and it gives us a blessing as its shadows flee away.

I. Then let us look at its dark side— involuntary sacrifice. How very dark it is! The constant suffering! The necessary pain! The inevitable sacrifice of beautiful, glorious life in innumerable ways, to sate the insatiable maw, not of *death*, but of other *life!*

It has been so from the beginning of earth's history. The rocks which we unearth today have their fossil remains, skeleton inside of skeleton, mute witnesses of what transpired on the primeval earth. Life everywhere fed upon life, one creature being sacrificed to keep another creature alive. And the same dark, mysterious spectacle is witnessed around us every hour. From the lowest form of insect life, through all grades of being up to man, we behold one preying upon another. Sometimes an insect carries about the germ of another attached to its back, that will in time take its life. We behold the feeble and the little sacrificed to the appetite of the large and the strong. Insects are consumed by other insects, by reptiles and by birds. The mouse and the sparrow are the ordained food of the hawk. The smaller fish are eaten by the larger. The lamb is the prey of the fox and the wolf. The kid is pounced upon by the eagle. The antelope is devoured by the leopard, and the lion and the tiger leap upon the ox. They all live by sacrificing each other and cannot live without it.

Man! he, too, lives by the slaughter of innocents, and the vastest and most costly sacrifices are made to satisfy his carnivorous appetites. Man in a real sense lives upon his fellowman. I refer not now to cannibalism, nor to the way in which human lives and human interests are often sacrificed to the selfish ambition, or the grasping avarice, or the cruel hate, or the devouring lusts of men. I refer only to the sacrifices made to the wants and necessities of others. You each live, day by day, because others sacrifice and suffer and die for you. You can scarcely help yourself even if you would; for dependence upon the sacrifice of some one is a necessity of civilized life.

As you sit with your family before the cheerful coal fire in the grate, did you ever once reflect that you have that blessing only because multitudes of men spend their lives underground in the depths of coal mines, covered with filth, and constantly exposed to pestilence and explosion and death? You travel over land and sea, and ship your goods and grain and cattle at a great speed; but the engineers and firemen and brakemen who drive the trains and handle the cars are prematurely cut off. Their lives are shortened to serve you. The man who blows the glass that lets the health-giving and cheerful light into your homes knows that the number of his days will be lessened. The metallic goods, gold and silver and plated, and steel and iron ware, are made by workmen who will sooner or later be killed by the dust they must inhale, and the necessary dangers of their occupations. I have seen the pale workmen making these goods, wearing sponges over their nostrils. But nothing wholly avails. You want the goods; they die to make them.

You go to your stores and buy beautiful fabrics and ready-made apparel. You marvel at their cheapness, but always want them a little cheaper. They are cheap—cruelly, wickedly cheap—because the work was undersold and underlet; undersold to you at the price of the cheap life-breath of suffering mortals—poor men and women compelled to labor by the necessities of their lot, and crushed to death by the competition and rivalry of trade while they stitched and embroidered for you, it was as Tom Hood wrote in his immortal poem:

"Stitch, stitch, stitch,
    In poverty, hunger and dirt,
  Sewing at once, with a double thread,
    A shroud as well as a shirt."

And so remember, with at least a little humane pity, when you buy and wear these wondrously cheap things—remember

"O men with sisters dear,
    O men with mothers and wives,
  It is not linen you're wearing out,
    But human creatures' lives."

The makers of certain kinds of lace must work in very dim light, and always go blind. In our great iron-mills, by an explosion or the bursting of a pot, men are often roasted alive by a great mass of molten metal. City policemen are shot down in the defense of other people's homes, and city firemen are often burned to death to keep the property of others from being burned. The pioneers of civilization cut down the forests, drain the swamps and the marshes, fight wild beasts and savages, and die doing it; but others who come after them enter into the fruits of their labors, and enjoy what they have wrought.

Probably a thousand men will lay down their lives for every mile of our isthmus canal; but the Nation wants it, the world needs it, and they die to give it to us. And so on endlessly.

We may, by Christian effort, alleviate this suffering somewhat, and thus mitigate some of the sternness of this law of sacrifice; but still it will remain, woven, dark and cruel though it seems to be, into the very fabric of our being, our progress, and our civilization.

II. Let us now consider the *voluntary* sacrifice. This is the brighter side. There is now something Divine in its purpose and holy in its results, and we are able, partially at least, to understand it. The generous, the unselfish, the pure, the holy, lavish themselves upon the base and the unthankful. They suffer in the sufferings of others, and stand between them and the normal results of their wrong-doing.

All our voluntary benevolent societies that labor among the poor and vicious, all our free hospitals and charitable institutions, our friendly inns, social settlements, temperance and missionary organizations, are so many proofs that the provident and the good are voluntarily bearing the burdens of the vicious. Somebody must cure these public evils that make society rotten. Somebody must rescue the children that are born in haunts of vice. Somebody must forget ease and self-indulgence, and put a precious home behind him and go after the drunkard, the criminal and the abandoned, or society is undone.

Yes, some, at times, must enter the ranks and brave their bosoms to the missiles of death, and consent to be mowed down by the privation and sickness of the camp that liberty may not perish, that nations may live.

And glorious as this patriotic sacrifice is, you can find

sweeter and quite as noble vicarious sacrifice in the quiet obscurity of home and daily life, unnoted of men, and appreciated by and known only to God.

There are parents caring for unworthy children, sitting with them through long days and weary night-watches in illness, bearing their needless sorrows in thankless sympathy and service, and agonizing over their wretched sins. I have known an elder sister, by far the most gifted mind in the family, to care for a sick mother for twelve long years, and care for the home and the father; and then she helped three brothers and a sister to an education, putting two of them through college, working for years from early morning till midnight to do it, her own mind and heart hungering for the opportunity, she was giving to them, until she was broken in health by the cruel strain. And then she was flung aside by those whom she had served. I sometimes think the shining sun looks upon nothing more Divine among men than such sister-love.

Now, you take all these noblest acts of benevolence, all these voluntary immolations of self for the good of others which human history affords, fashion them together into one harmonious whole, then lift them up into infinite exaltation, and you have none other than the Character of God Himself as He stands related to sinful and suffering man—the *God of vicarious sacrifice*, THE GOD OF LOVE.

III. We see in Jesus the interpretation and perfect illustration of this Divine law of sacrifice. Hear the blessed words of the text: "Jesus answered them, saying, The hour is come that the Son of man should be glorified. Verily, verily, I say unto you, except a grain of wheat fall into the ground and die it abideth alone: but if it die it bringeth forth much fruit. Now is my soul troubled. And what shall I say? Father, save me from this hour. But for this cause came I unto this hour. Father, glorify thy name." HERE, YOU SEE, IS THE INCARNATE GOD BOWING DOWN SUBMISSIVE TO HIS OWN SACRED LAW OF SACRIFICE. Not without the anguish and the struggle, not without the shrinking of soul which characterizes our own worthiest deeds; but yet He hesitates not. As the grain of wheat must abide alone except it be cast into the furrow and there perish, so, if He would save others, *Himself* he cannot save. But He *came* to save others. And, if it be possible, He will save them at whatever cost to Himself. He therefore keeps back the prayer, "Father, save me from this hour," which instinctively comes to His lips, and breathe out the petition, "Father, glorify thy name." He bows to the inevitable condition and makes the sacrifice.

Friends, from a human standpoint of vision, was ever a life so completely thrown away, so utterly lost? Taking into account the transcendent qualities which Jesus possessed, the keenness of intellect, the penetration, the foresight, the ability to read human nature, the sagacity, the magnetism, the force of character all of which he possessed in unequaled measure, and which He might have used to His own advantage, was ever life so thrown away? History does not afford the parallel of one who, with such matchless abilities and opportunities, so utterly squandered them, and was so completely bankrupted of results. By an easy use of His remarkable powers He might have acquired vast possessions; but He purposely became and remained so poor that He had not where to lay His head, often suffering from unappeased hunger, always eating the bread of charity, and redeemed only by love from abject want.

No other man could have so swayed the masses and created enthusiasm for himself; but He never did, and never tried to gain a permanent popular following. He might have handled the influential political leaders of His day, and lifted Himself to the summit of power; but He never sought their allegiance, or even made their acquaintance. He established no new school of philosophy, as other great minds before Him had done; He gained no popular influence; He wrote no books and left not even a line behind Him. He did not make or alter one law; He did not seat or unseat one ruler; He did not cast down one heathen altar, or break one poor slave's chain, or alter one custom. The religions of the world were, when He died, precisely what they were when He was born. The governments were as scheming, as corrupt, as tyrannous, as wicked. He was tried as a common criminal, and made no defense. He was put to death between two thieves, and all seemed utterly and disgracefully lost.

At that hour a thoughtful man might have likened His life to a comet of surpassing brilliancy which had suddenly and unexpectedly appeared from some unknown quarter of the heavens, attracted a brief attention, and then had as suddenly disappeared, to be as soon forgotten. No husbandman ever went into his field and sowed the grains of wheat more carelessly than did Jesus apparently throw His chances away. Was ever life so irretrievably lost? But, yet, with the halo of that cross lighting up the centuries, and destined, as we know, to yet flood the whole world with its light, we are able to add, WAS EVER LIFE SO GLORIOUSLY SAVED IN THE LOSING?

Ah! how supremely wise was the Redeemer's conduct, and how Divine His example! This outpouring of God's own life that others might have life and have it more abundantly! The great heart of love, "touched with a feeling of our infirmity" and beating in sympathetic pulsations with the fevered pulse of a suffering humanity! beholding our ruin and hasting to our redemption! It was the self-sacrificing love of God in full display, taking our place and suffering in our stead that you and I, my hearer, and all who will believe, might not perish.

And this was God's way to lift men. It was just then that God was glorified. No other act so became Him. The glory of creating sixty millions of worlds and suns was nothing in comparison! The moment of His extreme humiliation was the moment of supreme triumph. His death hour was the first hour of His reign as a redeeming God. Then was infinite love tested and found true. Then was infinite grace manifested. Then the anthem, "Worthy is the Lamb," began to be sung, and those hallelujahs of praise which shall continually rise and swell and roll on, in ever-increasing waves of melody, till Heaven and earth are full of His glory were first heard! And now notice:

IV. This is the law of godlikeness for us. Hear Jesus state it. "He that loveth his life shall lose it: and he that hateth his life in this world shall keep it unto life eternal. If any man serve me, let him follow me: him will my Father honor."

1. We can reach our own highest good only by a death to self. There is a something within us inherited from old Adam that is so infused into all our faculties that it becomes ourself. We may call this inheritance "depravity," or "the old man," or "the carnal mind," or "the law of sin and death." It matters not by what name it goes, it is a dark, diabolical, perverting thing. It corrupts the heart, perverts the sensibilities, defiles the imagination, drugs the conscience, weakens the will. "The whole head becomes sick and the whole heart faint." This vile infection so possesses every faculty that there is no moral soundness in us.

A human life thus defiled by this satanic virus is alienated from a life of love and a God of love. It does not take to godliness. It has a subtle affinity for evil, a trend downward, a propensity for sin and self-indulgence. It displays inordinate selfishness, regardless of the interests of others and the glory of God. Hence, Jesus said this self must die.

> "There is a foe of hidden power
>   The Christian well may fear.
>   More subtle far than outward sin,
>   And to the heart more dear.

It is the power of selfishness,
   The proud and willful I;
And ere my Lord can reign in me,
   My very *self* must die."

When a child of God fully consents to it and seeks the blessing with all his heart, this propensity to evil can be taken out by the baptism with the Holy Spirit. It was only subdued in regeneration; it was not destroyed. It was put down; it was not put out. It was held in with bit and bridle; but it is a troublesome, fiery steed, ready to run away with its driver at any moment. It pleads for its life; but it must be given over to die. In other words, the heart that has it must consent to die to all that the natural man holds dear, — die to all but holiness and God. When all is put on the altar for death, the heavenly fire will fall and consume the dross of the heart. The "old man" will die, and from his grave will come forth "the new man, created in righteousness and holiness of truth."

2. We must thus die to live in the largest usefulness. "Except the grain of wheat fall into the ground and die it abideth alone." It is the great Christian paradox, which Christ Himself so fully illustrated. Die to live; *lose* your life in order to *save* it. He who lives for himself only makes an utter failure of life. On the contrary, he who lives as if he hated life, who lays all the forces of his life on the altar of Jesus to be used in the service of God and humanity, HE KEEPS AND SAVES HIMSELF UNTO LIFE ETERNAL.

This is the essential condition and law of divinest usefulness. "If any man will serve me, let him follow me: and where I am there will also my servant be." Follow Jesus in the death of self-sacrifice, in His indifference to worldly honors, and His contempt for worldly riches and human applause. Follow Him to the firing line, where the cause of right is the most unpopular, and truth is shot at and stabbed by dagger tongues, and the battle is hottest for temperance and righteousness, for humanity and

God. Follow Him when others falter and fail, when others hiss and wag their tongues and curse goodness, and cry with the hate of Hell, "Crucify him, crucify him!" To follow Jesus then, through the judgment hall and over the *Via Dolorosa* and up the steeps of Calvary, while demons howl and rocks rend and darkness settles, and Goodness and Love are crucified, is to walk the path of honor and get the crown of final glory.

I entreat you who are young to learn this all-important lesson. You are not yet hardened by the deceitfulness of sin. You are deliberately adopting life-principles. On the one hand, you see men; all too numerous, who are grasping, selfish, ambitious, unscrupulous, eager to ride to place and power, and willing to crush anybody, and to sacrifice any human interest to do it. On the other hand, here is the perfect God-man, and all who would be like Him, giving themselves to the ministry of others. Which company will you join? The lesson of Jesus' life is this; *the path to the divinest and most enduring usefulness lies through the sepulchre where self-seeking is buried. Give thy life away if thou wouldst save it forever! In the meanest, over-reaching, selfishness, labor to make the most of thy little self; so shalt thou lose thy life, thy soul, thy all!*

Oh, how we need this lesson! And I thank God that more and more men are learning it. There are multitudes today who are poor because they would be honest and unselfish. They preferred usefulness to a large bank account, and riches of character to riches of purse. They have saved but little; yet they have saved conscience and truth and self-respect and love and faith—true manhood. They have comforted sorrow, and cured ignorance, and redeemed from vice, and made the lives of others better. They need none of your pity, for they have laid up abundance on high.

I have known a wife to live with a drunkard husband. For his sake and her children's she consented to be covered with shame and disgrace. She told me her parents did not know of her anguish. She had but to speak a word and her family would fly to her rescue; but she concealed her wretchedness and suffered on. And there are innumerable such wives and mothers who are martyrs to debauchery and dissoluteness, and who die daily for others. There are daughters who are sweetly pouring out their lives in the care of aged parents and thus are clothing themselves with the white robes of the saints.

There are some of God's purest who are sacrificing the enjoyments of home and health and strength and fortune to press upon the consciences of this guilty nation the moral reforms of the day. Others are sailing to foreign shores to carry the Gospel of Christ to thankless heathen; others still are giving of their very living to keep them there.

"Sarah Hosmer, of Lowell, Mass., though a poor woman, supported a student in the Nestorian Seminary, who became a preacher of Christ. Five times she gave fifty dollars, earning the money in a factory, and sent out five native pastors to Christian work. When sixty years old, she longed to furnish Nestoria with one more preacher of Christ; and, living in an attic, she took in sewing until she had accomplished her cherished purpose. In the hands of this consecrated woman, money transformed the factory girl and the seamstress into a missionary of the Cross, and then multiplied her six-fold." She died to live; and the story of her life is as fragrant as the alabaster box of ointment poured upon the head of Christ.

I know of women who have dedicated themselves to the care of half a hundred children apiece in orphanages, mothering the offspring of want and sin without other compensation than the smile of Christ. Others can be named who go from homes of abundance and culture and purity to fish fallen girls out of the purlieus of vice in our great cities. They have been fitly called the angels of the slums; and they are fitting themselves to be the companions of angels forever.

We might point to teachers and preachers in great numbers who are toiling faithfully and enthusiastically for a small fraction of the earthly compensation they might have gained in some other avocations. Gratitude should lead us to remember the men in the Cabinet of our Nation who have laid aside a professional income more than ten times greater than their pittance of a salary, that they may serve their country. And one of them, Secretary Hay, turned from the enjoyment of wealth and the sweets of literature and authorship, to serve his Nation and his age. He became the greatest diplomat of his times, but died prematurely, a sacrifice on the altar to bless mankind.

O, the spirit of Christ is abroad over the world. It is ennobling and sanctifying human hearts. Under its holy inspiration men are living and toiling, they are suffering and dying for others. At times some are troubled in soul like their Master before them, and cry, "How long, O Lord, how long?" He answers them: "Suffer child, and sacrifice a little longer." And they toil on for others, and lose life itself on their heaven-appointed Calvary. Then are they glorified. These are they that come up out of great tribulation, to wear crowns of usefulness and eternal victory. "He that saveth his life shall lose it:" he that gives it in sacrifice shall keep it unto life eternal. May God keep us all from the consuming canker of selfishness, and help us to give ourselves to the service of Christ and this dying world.

Sermon II
ETERNAL LIFE

John xvii.3: "And this is life eternal, that they should know thee the only true God, and him whom thou didst send, even Jesus Christ."

MAN INSTINCTIVELY CLINGS to existence and naturally covets life. This innate prompting inclines us to put a fanciful interpretation upon this wonderful passage of Scripture, in which Jesus touched the deepest depths of moral, sentient being. When the Master speaks of eternal life, the poor, halting, human thought catches only at the idea of continued *existence*, a *duration* of being unmeasured by the flight of years, untouched by the finger of dissolution. The *time* element in the Divine message fixes the attention with irresistible attraction, and all else is nearly lost sight of, if not quite forgotten.

It is because man generally shrinks from death and dislikes the thought of passing away. It piques us to think that there are birds of the air and beasts of the field of greater longevity than ourselves. The trees of the forest whose grateful shade we seek, cast their shadow upon our fathers' fathers, and our children's children will seek their shelter long after we are forgotten. The mountains lift their gigantic peaks to the heavens and look proudly down upon the pigmy race of mortals, whose duration, comparatively, is like the morning vapors that play about their summits for a little time and then vanish away.

You look upon the obelisk in Central Park, New York; it is startling to reflect that the little boy Moses played about it, and the eyes of the manly Joseph beheld it centuries before. We stand upon the beach of the ocean and listen to the voice of its mighty waters; but the same ocean sang the same dirge of wrecked fleets to other ears a hundred generations ago. The rivers that playfully toss our barks on their bosoms seem to sing with their rippling waves the words of Tennyson:

"Men may come, and men may go,
But we go on forever."

It disturbs man, the master of the world, the chiefest and best of earthly creations, to reflect that the inanimate things about him *abide*, while *he* must so soon pass away. And so he catches eagerly at the thought of *continued* existence, of *enduring* life.

But it is by no means certain that mere existence, even through interminable flights of years, irrespective of character or quality, would be an unmixed good, a thing to be desired, a prize to be coveted. Many a poor creature is so dazed by trouble and overwhelmed by sorrow as to pray for death. Not a day passes but some one, with suicidal hand, loosens the silver cord and breaks the golden bowl in the vain expectation that death will bring an escape from self in the oblivion of a dreamless, eternal sleep. What multitudes of lives are so full of shame and folly and consequent wretchedness as not to be worth living! How many, on account of the sin behind them and the woe before them, have infinitely more occasion than Job ever had to pray his prayer, "O, that I might have my request: and that God would grant me the thing that I long for! Even that it would please God to destroy me, that he would let loose his hand upon me and cut me off!"

All this Jesus knew full well, far better than mere mortal ever knew it: and so when He spoke of giving *eternal life* to all whom the Father had given Him, he immediately explains what eternal life is, that all the world might understand that it was not merely unceasing existence. "And this is life eternal that they might know thee, the only true God, and Jesus Christ whom thou didst send." Oh, blessed parenthesis in the perfect prayer that flashes such a light upon the true destiny of man! Life is more than existence, thank God! else might we all sing the atheistic song:

"Count all the joys that thou hast seen;
Count all the tears from anguish keen;
And know, whatever thou hast seen,
'Twere better never to have been."

This leads me then to consider,

I. What this eternal life is which God's Word so exalts and teaches us to prize.

Jesus, from whose word there can be no appeal, tells us plainly that it is to KNOW GOD, and to KNOW CHRIST. It was for this, then, that man was created in the Divine image and made a living soul, that he might "know God." This is the highest possible attainment of any creature—his consummate life—to "know God." This is the great end which the Christian religion sets before us, the sum of all good, the crown of all blessedness—to" know God."

But let us not be careless now. This is a superficial age. Our reading is superficial, our thinking, our convictions, our very religion—the thing of all things that ought to be deep and genuine—is too commonly a thing of opinions and profession and form and fashion, that does not go down into the deeps of the heart-life.

We may well pause and reflect upon this wonderful statement. There are so many kinds of knowledge! It must be some peculiar kind that can be called by the Master Himself eternal life. For instance, it can not be a mere intellectual *belief* in or admission of the existence of God. It is not a mere apprehension that there is such a being with certain qualities and attributes. Nor is it a cold, philosophical speculation *about* Him; nor yet a formal knowledge of what He has said of Himself. It is such a knowledge of God as involves a *union* with Him, a living, conscious possession of fellowship with Him, so that we are *"in Him,"* and one with Him in spirit and life.

The difference between these two kinds of knowledge can be illustrated in many ways. Suppose a man has been brought up to be a drunkard from a child. He takes a scientific work on the deleterious influences of alcohol on the human system. He there learns how it deranges the stomach, and every vital organ; how it injures and hardens the brain; how it perverts the appetite and arouses the passions; how it gives to every drop of blood an open mouth that clamors for drink; how it burns up man, body and soul. He there learns, also, by contrast, the superiority of a life of total abstinence over a life of intemperance. The man commits every statement in the book to memory, and can pass examination on every page. But there he stands, a bloated, beastly, diseased, half-drunken debauchee. What does he know after all about a life of temperance? He knows it intellectually, out of the book; but he does not know it actually, experimentally, at all. He has had no experience of a life of sobriety; of what it is to have a steady eye and a clear brain, an undiseased, underanged body, he knows nothing whatever.

Two persons enter a concert-room and listen to the same sacred oratories rendered by a noble company of artists. One has trained his ear till it is sensitive to harmony and delicately appreciative of every exquisite modulation of sound. His mind and judgment also are cultured, and the great theme of the almost-inspired composer is grasped and permitted to take possession of his being. His heart, too is touched by the Spirit of God, and brought into sympathy with the words of Holy Writ to which the music is set. He listens— listens with bated breath and suffused eye and thrilled heart, as waves of inspiring melody roll in upon his spirit and carry him, as it were, on a swelling tide of rapture into the very presence of the living God. But the other person has neither a musical ear, nor a cultured mind, nor a spiritual heart: he listens to the same sounds and hears what? Only noise, noise, noise, of which he soon wearies, and begins to whisper and chatter silly nothings of his empty mind like a magpie. Now, the two persons, in one sense, heard the same. yet, Oh, how much one heard that the other *did* not, *could* not hear!

Two persons read the same poem. The mind of one comes into sympathy with the author, sees his visions, and feels the power and beauty of his thoughts, and his deepest feelings and emotions are stirred, as he lives over again what the master-mind lived when he wrote. The other person reads the same lines and speaks the same words; but to him they are cold and dead. He sees nothing and feels nothing—not even the dullness and deadness of his own impoverished mind.

A Christian artist looks upon Raphael's *Transfiguration*. To him the immortal painting is almost a living scene. He feels the majesty of the conception, appreciates the harmony of the coloring, the beauty of outline, the skill of every touch; and as he looks upon the face of Jesus, his heart moves within him, and he feels like bowing down in reverent worship. But another comes along with so little of the artist's nature in him that he looks upon the same canvas with lack-luster eye and unkindled spirit, and then turns away in utter unconcern.

A man can repeat the twentieth chapter of Exodus without mistake, the ten commandments and all; but he is a blasphemer and a Sabbath-breaker and a thief and a liar and a murderer. The moral law has made no more impression on his soul than it did upon the tables of stone which Moses dashed to the earth. Oh, how unlike is his spirit to that of the great law-giver, who loved and revered God's commands as if they had been graven on his very heart by the finger of God.

Now, if these illustrations have not failed, you will perceive from them how very different is the formal knowledge of the intellect from that vital *heart* knowledge which enters into the experience and becomes life. You see how different persons hear and read and see and know the same things; yet the one class receives nothing, while the other is *taught* and *thrilled* and *inspired* and *transformed*.

In precisely these different ways do men know God. Some know that He is, know His attributes and moral qualities and will and Word; and yet they do not know Him. It is all intellectual and external to their real selves; it is not vital and transforming; it does not shape and control and possess the heart. They are still practically as those "who have no hope and are without God in the world."

But others know God, Oh, so differently! know Him with a knowledge that lights and comforts and guides and inspires their hearts evermore. They know Him as a Father; and their reverent hearts reach out to Him the hand of filial love, as children who should say in confidence and trust:

"The way is dark, my Father. Cloud on cloud
   Is gathering thickly o'er my head, and loud
   The thunders roar above me. See, I stand
   Like one bewildered. Father, take my hand,
   And through the gloom lead safely home Thy child."

Again, they know Him as a God of love, who plans in mercy and provides in grace; who watches over His children with untold tenderness; who does for them what is wisest and best. And knowing this they rest, in perfect peace, in the all-enfolding arms of Infinite Love.

Again, they know Him as an infinitely holy God, who hates sin with an unutterable hatred; and they, too, begin to love righteousness and to hate iniquity for the sake of Him whom their soul loveth. They begin to battle with temptation and to oppose evil. Aye, they seek the heart-cleansing work of the Holy Ghost in their hearts. And so their knowledge of God becomes vital and vitalizing. In countless ways it affects them for good and brings them into harmony with Him. They are lifted up out of their sinful groveling into a career of victory over sin, and endless growth in grace and spiritual exaltation. As the sap comes out of the earth into the tree, and, in some mysterious way, becomes wood and leaf and flower and fruit, so this true knowledge of God becomes, in the receptive and friendly heart, a transforming power; becomes conduct, yea, *life*, the beginning of life eternal.

As the sunlight falls from Heaven upon the flowers and paints their petals with the hues of the morning, so the knowledge which God imparts of Himself to willing hearts somehow clothes them with a Divine beauty and a tender grace not otherwise their own.

In like manner, also, said the Master, is the knowledge of *Jesus Christ* eternal life. The knowledge of Jesus, the incarnate God, the Redeemer, the atoning Savior; this, too, is eternal life. But how different may be the knowledge of Jesus which different men entertain! Judas and John walked alike with Jesus in unchecked, unrestrained intimacy for above three years. But how different was the knowledge of the selfish, cold-hearted traitor from that of the disciple who leaned on Jesus' bosom and drank so deeply the spirit of His love! One of the noblest, uninspired tributes ever paid to Jesus was written by the infidel Rousseau; but how widely different was his knowledge of the great being he praised from that of the Apostle Paul, to whom "to live was Christ;" who ate and drank and waked and slept, who preached and wrote and toiled and suffered and died for his Master; and who knew no life apart from Him! Robert Ingersol had more Christian training when a child than Dwight Moody, and each knew Jesus in his own way. But how different is the knowledge of the prayerless, sneering infidel from that of the flaming evangel of the cross whose life is prayer, who *thinks* and *talks* and *writes* and *lives* only for his Savior!

There is a knowledge of Jesus, like the knowledge of Socrates, or any other historic character, which leaves the will unsubdued, and the passions unchecked, and the heart untouched. But, Oh, there is a knowledge of Jesus which captures and captivates the soul, which melts the proud heart into submission, which calls out the most trustful, childish faith in Him as a Savior from sin.

There is a knowledge of Jesus which brings the soul to the cross, where faith in the shed blood, and the joy of forgiving love, and the peace of conscious pardon are found together. There is a knowledge of Jesus which basks in the sunshine of His affection, and walks in His light day by day; which finds in Him all needed inspiration; which looks to Him for all needed help and guidance; which knows no wish, and cherishes no desire, and forms no purpose aside from His sweet will.

Yes, there is a knowledge of Jesus obtained in the Pentecostal chamber. The adoring soul falls at His feet, not merely as One who died for our sins, but as One who lives to perform His high-priestly office and baptize the seeking, waiting heart with the Holy Ghost and fire. It is this baptism which cleanses the heart from inbred sin, and brings enduement of power for service, and swings one out into "the life more abundant," "the fullness of the blessing of the gospel of Christ."

Such knowledge of Jesus is *life*, the sweetest, purest, highest, holiest life that is possible to man. Yea, such knowledge is life eternal; for, linking as it does the human with the Divine, it makes man too good and too godlike to ever die. And now

II. We can see that the knowledge of God and Christ LEADS to life eternal. This knowledge is not only the thing itself, but it is also THE WAY to it.

This is the way in which Christ gives eternal life, by giving us a knowledge of God. And this is the way in which we receive it, by sitting as a pupil at Jesus' feet and learning of God. Whoever would have eternal life, let him go to school to the Son of God; let him seek night interviews with Him as Nicodemus did; let him wait upon Jesus, and serve Him, and drink in His spirit, as did the beloved disciple. Let him learn the infinite depths of compassion and charity and mercy for suffering, sinful fellow-mortals which characterized the Savior. Let him learn of the Redeemer the nobility of self-sacrifice, the joy of dying to self that others may live. Let him learn from the Holy One what it is to be one with God in complete submission to His will, unattracted and unstained by the evils of a sinful world.

The gaining of such knowledge is the gaining of eternal life, with all the unutterable blessedness which it involves. The adjusting of the heart and life to such knowledge is entering into the kingdom of Heaven, is finding the pearl of greatest price, the richest and best possible gift of God. "Whosoever findeth it findeth life."

Seek it, ye sin-laden, troubled ones, who long for the peace that passeth understanding, and the rest which the world cannot give: seek with teachable heart the great Master. Knock at the portals of this Divine knowledge and ye shall enter in and find rest to your souls.

I close with two remarks:

1. Heaven, for which the sorrowing world hath ever been longing, which imagination hath wrought upon, and fancy hath lovingly pictured, is a condition, a state of heart no less than a place. We dream of a realm far away, with walls and towers and gates of pearl and streets of gold, and mansions and harps and crowns and a throne; and our heaven is an earthly picture of Oriental, barbaric splendor. How much of this may enter into the reality we cannot know. But would it not be more real and more helpful to think of the abode of the blessed as being anywhere with God, and Heaven's reward as knowing God as He is, and being *with* Him and *like* Him?

Oh, to live through endless ages of ever-increasing knowledge and enjoyment of God! to unroll and fathom the mysteries of His love which we have long desired to look into! to stand with angels and glorified saints and look upon the new displays of Divine goodness and the fresh revelations which God shall make of Himself—ah! that will be *blessedness*, that will be *life*, that will be HEAVEN forever and ever!

2. We learn that Heaven begins here; that eternal life has the first flush of its morning dawn here in this present mortal life. This it is—to know God and Jesus Christ His Son—a knowledge that begins now, or is never gained. As the years roll on it will be ever deeper and wider and fuller. Budding *now*, it will have its perfect flower and fruitage in the eternal world. But it must begin *here*. Oh, *let* it begin here and now. Let this be the springtime of the eternal summer, the seed-time of learning God and Christ, which shall prelude the eternal harvest of knowing God *as He is*, and the blessedness of being forever like Him.

Sermon III
NOT ASHAMED OF THE GOSPEL
Preached Before the State Association of the Congregational Churches of Pennsylvania

Rom. i.16: "For I am not ashamed of the gospel; for it is the power of God unto salvation."

IN THESE DAYS OF GOSPEL TRIUMPHS, the boldness and full significance of this assertion can scarcely be appreciated. Only as we divest ourselves of nearly everything that has made us what we are, our surroundings, our age, our civilization, the marvelous history of the Christian centuries, and, by an effort of the mind, put ourselves back in Paul's age and in the place of one to whom he wrote, can we take in the moral sublimity of this utterance.

It was the age of a gilded, glorious heathenism, waning in its power and corrupt in its influence. Paul was writing to the Romans, the inhabitants of the capital city of the world—Rome, the seat of universal empire, the residence of statesmen, poets, philosophers, artists, historians, commanders; the seat of science and literature. It was the abode of men whose thought was philosophy and learning, whose speech was eloquence and song—men, the splendor of whose genius shed new luster on the city and nation and race, and filled the world with fame.

It was an age and place of enormous wealth existing side by side with the most abject and distressing poverty. Around carved marble palaces, resplendent with purple and silver and gold and gems, wandered hundreds of wretched slaves and troops of naked mendicants who made a trade of their poverty, and lived in discontented idleness and disgusting dependence on the grudging liberality of their patrons.

It was also an age at once of atheism and superstition. The services of religion were performed with most imposing ritualistic splendor; but all heart faith in religion was dead and gone. Gifted poets preferred the favor of rich but contemptible patrons to the smile even of Jupiter, and philosophers openly sneered at the puerile legends of the old mythologies. "The common worship was regarded," says Gibbon, "by the people as equally true, by the philosophers as equally false, and by the magistrates as equally useful." Seneca wrote: "We shall so adore all that ignoble crowd of gods which long superstition has heaped together, as to remember that their worship has more to do with custom than with reality." In short, nearly everything in the realm of religion was a matter of pomp and show, false, hollow and heartless.

It was also an age of intense pleasure-seeking, of boundless luxury, of horrible cruelty, and of sadness and gloom. The rabble that thronged the crowded streets wanted nothing but bread and the sports of the circus and the amphitheatre. But the Roman lords and their women vied with each other in the race of splendor, and plunged headlong into conscienceless extravagance. Ancient Roman simplicity and dignity and self-respect and lofty honor were no more. Fortunes were staked on the throw of a dice. A banquet would cost the price of a vast estate. Fish were brought from far-off shores; birds from Parthia and Ethiopia; single dishes were made of the brains of peacocks and the tongues of nightingales. "Countries were pillaged," says Farrar, and nations were crushed that an Apicius might dissolve pearls in the wine he drank, or that Lollia Paulina might gleam in a second-best dress of emeralds and pearls which had cost forty million sesterces. And side by side with this zest for pleasure was a heartless cruelty, sickening to contemplate. Whole menageries of beasts and regiments of men fought together in the arena to the delight of the populace. Capital punishments were by public crucifixion. Doomed martyrs were covered with pitch and set fire to, that their shirt of flame might light the public gardens. Masters and mistresses could inflict a death punishment upon their slaves with no one to call them to account; and a wanton and senseless barbarity often converted a household into a pandemonium, resounding with the blows of the scourging, the shrieks of the tortured, and the groans of the dying.

For an unavoidable mistake or mishap, or a venial fault—a cough, a sneeze, or the breaking of a dish—a Roman might fall into a frenzy of rage, and order his slave to be thrown to the beasts. Even a matron, for the misplacing of a jewel, or a displeasing arrangement of a tress of hair, might fly into a fury of anger and order her slave to be lashed or crucified. In fashionable society nothing was calm and natural. It was either a deluge of wasting dissipations and turbid pleasure, or a seething cauldron of vices, or a fierce conflagration of malignant passions!

And over the abnormal social life of heartless self-seeking, there hung clouds of gloom and the darkness of despair. Life was so intense that it was unendurable; yet men dreaded death, for their philosophies and religions utterly failed to light the mystery that enveloped the grave. And scarcely ever did a great Roman live out the measure of his days and die in peace. It was either assassination or suicide: If others spared him he fled for refuge from his own crimes or sorrows to a self-inflicted death, with a mock courage which was ill-disguised despair. Of this age Juvenal exclaimed in a burst of sadness: "Posterity will add nothing to our immorality; our descendants can but do and desire the same crimes as ourselves." And Seneca wrote: "All things are full of iniquity and vice; more crime is committed than can be remedied by restraint. We struggle in a huge contest of criminality; daily the passion for sin is greater, the shame in committing it is less. Wickedness is no longer committed in secret: it flaunts before our eyes, and has been sent forth so openly into public sight, and has prevailed so completely in the breast of all, that *innocence is not rare*, BUT NON-EXISTENT!"

Friends, it was to such a Roman world as this that Paul wrote: "I am not ashamed of the gospel of Christ." And at the time of writing, remember, Paul was not a verdant youth of visionary expectations, of ardent impulses, of feeble intellect, of slender understanding, and little knowledge of the world. Twenty-five years before he had an enviable reputation among the great lawyers of his nation; and for twenty-two years he had been one of the pillars of the Christian Church, *the* great apostle to the Gentiles, without a peer in ability and usefulness, blessed beyond all others with visions and revelations of God. It was such a man, sobered by experience, in the zenith of his powers, who calmly proposed to enter Rome the Babylon of iniquity, the huge bayou of reeking corruption, the awful aggregation of all earth's wickedness, and conquer it and purify it with an application of the simple Gospel of Christ. Now let us consider

I. What Paul meant by "the Gospel of Christ." It will not do for us to theorize here at the outset of this discussion. Paul shall be his own interpreter. He meant a DIVINE CHRIST; for to these same Romans he spake of "Christ who is over all God blessed forever." Again he meant an ATONING CHRIST; for, explaining his preaching to the Corinthians, he wrote: "I declare unto you the gospel which I preached unto you, how that Christ died for our sins."

Again it was the Gospel of a CRUCIFIED Christ; for he wrote: "I determined not to know anything among you save Jesus Christ and him crucified." Furthermore, it was a Gospel of salvation that was conditioned on the acceptance and belief of the soul; for he says: "The gospel of Christ was the power of God unto salvation to everyone that believeth," and "we are saved by faith." Moreover, he preached a gospel of salvation from eternal death; for he wrote: "The Lord Jesus shall be revealed from heaven with his mighty angels, taking vengeance on them that know not God and that obey not the gospel of our Lord Jesus Christ, who shall be punished with everlasting destruction."

Still further; his Gospel did not hint at a second probation for the heathen, for he wrote to these same Romans that the heathen are "without excuse," for "God manifested" his truth even "unto them," and they deliberately "refused to have God in their knowledge:" therefore, "As many as have sinned without law shall also perish without law... in the day when God shall judge the secrets of men according to my gospel by Jesus Christ." And what is more, he taught the doctrine of SANCTIFICATION as a second work of grace, wrought in the heart in this life by the Spirit of God. He wrote to these same Romans about "being sanctified by the Holy Ghost," and prayed for the members of the Church in Thessalonica: "Now the God of peace himself sanctify you wholly, and I pray God your whole spirit and soul and body be preserved blameless unto the coming of our Lord Jesus." In his epistles to the churches, and his sermons, he has seventy-five verses that teach this second blessing.

To be sure, Paul had not studied Theology at Andover, Mass., and might not have received the latest revelations on these subjects. But he took his theological course during his three years tarrying in Arabia, communing with Jesus and the Holy Ghost; and I am simply pointing out the truths which he calls "my gospel," of which he declares, "I am not ashamed."

And once more, he held up everywhere what some of our modern finical, fastidious, super-refined preachers and teachers are pleased to call "the gross and gory theory of the atonement." Fifteen times in his epistles he lays supreme stress upon "the blood of Christ." "We have peace through the blood of his cross." "We are made nigh by the blood of Jesus." Our "consciences are purged by the blood of Christ." The "Church is purchased with his blood." "God hath set forth Jesus Christ to be a propitiation through faith in his blood." "We have redemption through his blood," and are "now justified by his blood."

This, my brethren, was the system of truth with which Paul proposed to assault the wickedness of the heathen world. He had no confidence in glowing oratory, or brilliant rhetoric, or subtle philosophy, or uncorrupted humanitarian schemes. If he had used the word "Gospel," in the sense in which some use it today, meaning by it gushing philanthropy and goody-goody sentimentalism; if he had intended by it merely fine-spun theories about the unity of God, and an overruling providence, and immutable distinctions between right and wrong, and the golden rule of equity, and the doctrine of the immortality of the soul, he would never have dreamed of saying: "I am not ashamed of the gospel of Christ."

It was not at any of these things that the brilliant literati and cultured heathen philosophers scoffed and derided. O, no: he went to them with the story of a Divine Savior, walking the earth in the form of a man, and dying on the cross between two thieves, a sacrifice for the sins of the world, only by whose atoning blood could the most cultured heathen be saved from everlasting death. It was *this* gospel, to the Jew a stumbling block, to the Greeks foolishness, to the haughty Romans an offense, and revolting to human nature everywhere and always, of which Paul was not ashamed.

With it, as a Christian Hercules, he dared to attempt to cleanse the Augean stables of Rome, to smite the heathen gods, and make the oracles dumb. By its divine power he expected to assault the principalities and powers of the wickedness of this world, and overturn all the powers of darkness, and bring in the universal kingdom of Christ, wherein shall dwell righteousness. And when the unbelieving world lifted its jeers and shouts of derision at this sublime scheme of Paul, in the strength of his heaven born faith he answered back: "I am not ashamed of the gospel of Christ."

II. I call your attention to the fact that unlike Paul, *some are* ashamed of it.

1. For instance, there are those who reject the fundamental doctrine of the *cross*. Some of these deny the depravity and utter sinfulness of man that made the cross an awful necessity, and belittle the crucifixion into a mere *incident* or *accident* in the earthly life of Jesus, instead of being an event necessary and chosen and predetermined from before the foundation of the world. There are those who deny the *Divinity of Jesus*, and thus make His death of no more worth or potency than the death of Socrates; who deny that His death was vicarious — He dying in our stead, and that it was an expiation, removing our guilt (exposure to punishment), and that it was propitiatory, satisfying the awful holiness of God and the public justice of the moral universe; who deny

that it was even necessary to preserve the honor and integrity of God's law and government.

Now, men who reject these truths simply cut the very heart out of the Gospel and rob it of its convicting and converting power. It will not do to call these mere theories of men, and so waive them aside as unessential and immaterial, They are the very essence of the truth as it is in Jesus, the very warp and woof of the Gospel. Dr. Henry Smith is clearly right when he says: "The very nature of the sufferings and death of Christ is that they are an expiation for sin. This is the very idea of a sacrifice. It is its exhaustive definition: it is the thing itself, and not a deduction or inference from it. THIS IS THE FACT, and not a theory about it," Now when men deliberately set at naught these truths that God has stated over and over again, they are making the cross of Christ of none effect; they are subliminating it into thin air, as powerless as a weak speculation or an idle tale. They are practically putting themselves among the number of those who are ashamed of the Gospel of Christ

2. Again, there are those who ignore the *conditions of salvation* revealed in the Gospel. Jesus saw men flocking around Him, and said unto them: "If any man will come after me, let him *deny himself,* and take up his *cross* daily and *follow me."*

Paul declared that his ministry in Ephesus had consisted in teaching publicly and from house to house, "repentance toward God and faith toward our Lord Jesus Christ." To these same Ephesians he wrote that "Christ loved the church, and gave himself up for it that he might sanctify it, having cleansed it… that he might present the church to himself a glorious church, not having spot or wrinkle or any such thing; but that it should be holy and without blemish." These hard, sharp, inexorable conditions of eternal life, and descriptions of it, are not agreeable, and never can be pleasing to the carnal heart.

Now when religious teachers or preachers dislike these divinely revealed conditions of life, and hunt around for other and easier terms of salvation that prick the conscience less, and do not humble the proud will, nor break the hard heart, nor lessen the attachment to sin, they are simply preaching *another* gospel which is not a gospel. Sin is inconceivably wicked, a causeless rebellion, infinitely insulting and offensive to God, and the atoning Savior is the only ground of hope, the only source of life. "The carnal mind is enmity against God, for it is not subject to the law of God, neither indeed can be." The "old man" is the essence of the devil, the spirit of Hell, and the only remedy for it is the sin-killing, heart-cleansing baptism with the Holy Spirit. To adopt any slight, minimizing, apologetic conceptions of sin as a triviality, an infirmity, a necessity, or a negative side of good, "good in the making," and to applaud morality and culture and self-development as any sort of remedy for it, is to belie the whole Gospel. The preacher in the pulpit who does it, or the man in the pew who wants him to do it, is of the number of those who are ashamed of the Gospel of Christ.

3. There are all those who distrust the Gospel as an all-sufficient power to elevate men, and seek to bolster it up by props and helps and additions, hoping thus to add to its efficacy. At the time Paul wrote his epistle to the Romans, heathenism had a most elaborate ritual and highly attractive religious services. All that art could do had been done to redeem paganism from vulgarity, and cover up its deformities, and make it beautiful to the eye, and pleasing to men. There were no less than fifty-one legal religious festivals observed annually at Rome with all conceivable pomp and splendor. There were lustrations, processions, festivals and formal prayers for all occasions of life. As James Freeman Clark has observed, "As the old faith *died* more ceremonies were added; for as life goes out, forms come in. As the winter of unbelief lowers the

stream of piety, the ice of ritualism accumulates along its banks. " Religion became more and more a charm, on the exact performance of which the favor of the gods depended; so that ceremonies were sometimes performed thirty times before the essential accuracy was attained.

Now, Christianity had absolutely nothing of form and ceremony with which to displace all this gorgeous ritualism of the heathen world. The worship of the early Christians was simplicity itself. They never thought of a ritualistic service until after the decadence of their piety. The entire religious service of Paul and the disciples of his time consisted of the two sacraments of baptism and the Lord's supper, singing and prayer, the expounding of Scripture, and the proclamation of the Gospel of Christ.

It was by this simple instrumentality that Paul proposed to conquer the heathen world, and he declared that he was not ashamed of his means. When I think of the multiplied sacraments, and the attitudinizing of the gorgeously robed priests of the Roman Catholic Church, their tinkling bells and smoking censers and sprinkling of holy water, and crucifixes and candles and positions and manmillenery, and when I see nearly all of this repeated in the Episcopal service, I am filled with sorrow, and feel in my inmost soul that the evidence is painfully abundant that many church dignitaries have gone a long step backward, and have lost confidence in the conquering power of the simple Gospel of Christ.

And when I see ministers and churches resorting to all manner of devices and expedients, and questionable, catch-penny enterprises for the sake of securing patronage and support, I cannot help feeling that it evinces a lack of confidence in the majesty of the Gospel as abundantly able to subdue the world.

4. There are those who rail at all creeds as man-made, unneeded, and out of place in the economy of the church of our day. Many are ready to tell you that they are be-

gotten of bigotry and ignorance, and born in darkness,
an inheritance of past years wholly out of place in our
glorious era. "Why not," they say, "take the Bible as our
declaration of faith and be content?" There is something
seemingly so meek and pious and Scriptural, and apparently so clever, in all this clamor, that multitudes are captured by it. I confess I know of no talk more puerile. Accept the Bible as our system of faith! Indeed! But whose
interpretation of it? Who does not know that there is an
allegorical interpretation of the Bible, and a mystical, and
a rationalistic, and a spiritualistic, and a Catholic, and a
Unitarian, and a Universalian, as well as an orthodox
interpretation, and that some of these are as widely sepa-
rated as Heaven and earth?

What is a creed, anyway, but a fair and ample statement of the truths of the Gospel as understood by those
who adopt it? Any church or body of churches owes it to
its membership, owes it to the public, owes it to the age
in which it lives, and owes it to God, to distinctly avow its
belief. To do otherwise is to shirk duty and to deal dis-
honestly with men.

Those who sneer at creeds and belittle formulas of
faith are taking a position anti-biblical, and anti-com-
mon-sense. The Christian religion deals with the grav-
est problems of human existence, and human destiny.
It is based on the positive revelation of God's will to
men. The Bible is the most positive of all books. It is
utterly against a "go-as-you-please," "believe-what-
you-will," "happy-go-lucky," superficial, trifling life.
Christ was the most positive of all teachers. His greatest apostle, Paul, in the fervor of his devotion to the
truth, exclaims: "Though an angel from heaven should
preach unto you any gospel other than that which we
preached unto you, let him be anathema."

How utterly unlike them are these theological bant-
lings who sail on a wild sea of speculation without an-

chor, chart, or compass— who advocate a "go-as-you-please," believe-what-you-will" system of doctrine; who are theologically all things to all men, if by any means they can drum up a following! Such teachers have no permanent and lasting influence for good; for abiding influence is born of conviction. Such churches have no element to bind their membership together in lasting union. They are only a social conglomeration of disconnected individuals, called together by an accident, to be scattered when the accident is gone.

An ample creed, honestly adopted, is a mighty power. It furnishes the basis of a spiritual education of the youth. It builds the individual believer on the everlasting rock. It binds the churches together into a common body of Christ, all alike feeding upon His truth, and animated by His Spirit, and united in the common work of bringing the world to Christ. To sneer at creeds is only a cowardly way of sneering at the everlasting truths which they represent; and to be ashamed of them is to be ashamed of the Gospel of the Son of God.

5. Those also who favor lowering the standard of admission to the church, who, in the name of the Master, cater to the world and bid for its support, and seek its applause, are simply exhibiting a secret dislike for the Gospel conditions of salvation and the Gospel type of piety. In short, the yoke of the Master has grown irksome to them; His life is no longer their chosen model, and they are ashamed of the Gospel of Christ.

III. Let us consider *why* Paul was not, and why we should not be, ashamed of the Gospel. "It was," said he, "the power of God unto salvation to every one that believeth." Perhaps I can best illustrate how the Gospel was a power, and what kind of a power it was, by a quotation or two. In one of his poems Lucretius declared that *faith in the gods* had been the curse of the race, and that immortality was a silly delusion. The elder Pliny wrote:

"All religion is the offspring of necessity, weakness and fear. What God is, if in truth he be anything distinct from the world, it is beyond the compass of man's understanding to know. But it is a foolish delusion which has sprung from human weakness and human pride, to imagine that such an infinite being would concern himself with the affairs of men. The vanity of man and his insatiable longing after existence have led him also to dream of a life after death. A being full of contradictions, he is the most wretched of creatures. Man is full of desires and wants that reach to infinity, and can never be satisfied. His nature is a lie, uniting the greatest poverty with the greatest pride. Among these so great evils, the best thing God has bestowed on man is the power to take his own life!"

These statements flash a calcium light upon the awful spiritual condition of the Roman world. The masses were sunk in a rayless abyss of moral degradation; and even the cultured, the refined, the truly noble had lost all faith in God, all sense of the dignity of man, and all prospects for the future. They were actually living "without hope and without God in the world."

Now, the first element of power in the Gospel was, that it brought to men an assurance of a God, and the true conception. He was not one of the ignoble rabble of gods that filled Rome; He was not even another heartless Jove whose chief mission was to hurl thunderbolts, and who could look on unmoved while men were swept to death like so many flies. This God was in infinite Father, infinitely wise and good, with a heart of infinite compassion, and mercy, and justice and love. And not only so; He was an *atoning* God, a *self-sacrificing* God, carrying the sorrows of the world on His heart, and uniting Himself to man by an incarnation that He might bear our sins, and die in our stead, and open a fountain of mercy for the race. Think you there was no *power* in such a revelation as that? A morning sun never smote a fog-bank with more power than this truth smote the deism that floated over the Roman world like a malaria of death.

A second element of power in the Gospel was that it taught the grandeur and infinite worth of the human soul. What must be the infinite dignity of a nature for which the infinite God puts forth all the resources of His mighty love, for which the Son of God could die upon the cross? If such a sacrifice were meet and proper, then an inconceivable significance attaches to man. When the Gospel came the heathen world had been so drenched by human gore shed in wars, in the cruel sports of the arena, by assassination, and infanticide and suicide, that all sense of the worth of man as man was becoming extinguished from the human breast. When a Roman babe was born, and the nurse announced it to the father, if he deigned to give it a kindly look, it was understood that the child was welcomed and it was allowed to live. But if he turned away with a look of displeasure, the babe was quietly smothered to death as an unwelcome comer to the world.

Not until the incarnate God crossed the threshold of this earth in the stable at Bethlehem, did the worth of a babe dawn upon the mind of man. Not until the price of man's redemption was paid on Calvary did he have the faintest conception of the value of the soul.

And in Christ men not only found their worth but also their immortality. If their significance was to be estimated by the sorrow of an infinite God, then surely this earthly horizon did not bound their existence. The stage of time on which man was playing his little part had for its background ETERNITY. Immortality was not a vain conceit and a tantalizing dream, but a blessed reality. In Jesus he saw the surety of life beyond death.

Now, think you, it was a small thing to go to the despairing philosopher with such a Gospel as that? Was it nothing to tell the homesick captive of war that he had a home beyond the skies? Nothing to tell the meanest, down-trodden, half-starved slave in Rome that he was a redeemed child of God! Nothing to tell a wretched gladiator who must die a death of violence tomorrow in the amphitheatre that he was or might be by faith a *Son of God* and an *heir of immortality!* There are no words to describe the change wrought in their conception of themselves by this Gospel. It brought inspiration, incentive, joy, courage, betterment, hope. It was like a gale of wind to becalmed mariners; like a morning of peace after a night of anguish on a stormy deep, like awaking in safety after a sleep of horrid nightmare and frightful dreams.

Nor was this all. This Gospel had in it the power to reform Roman society. If God was the common Father of all, and Christ died for all, then all are brothers of equal privilege and common destiny. Send such a truth as that to Rome in the glowing heart of Paul, and see how it would humble the haughty oppressor and bring the proud master low; while it would give dignity and importance to the meanest slave, and lift the down-trodden and lowly incalculably in the scale of being.

This Gospel helped every man to find himself. Each could see his sin as blacker, and feel his burden of guilt as heavier than ever before. But over against his ill-desert was set an offer of pardon and a door of hope. Each could, for the first time, find in Christ, at once an interpreter and an *ideal,* a condemnation and an inspiration.

Just as the young Roman painter did not know his own genius until he gazed, entranced, upon the great masterpiece which revealed all the power of the pencil, when he cried out in a glow of emotion, "I, too, am a painter," so a human soul may touch all other heroes, sound the depths of philosophies, try all other religions; but until it stands face to face with the Lord of the race, the Savior of the lost, it knows not, it cannot know, it feels not, it cannot feel, either its own unworthiness, its own boundless capacities, or its own supreme destiny. The hour when Christ is revealed to the mind and heart, is the hour when the soul realizes what it is, and what it may become. Here are felt the woes of sin; here are found the highest motives; here are received the holiest inspirations.

Paul realized all this. He had seen the gospel tried. He knew that it had a Divine power, universal in its application and permanent in its results. And, therefore, he exclaimed with a courage born of certain knowledge, "I am not ashamed of the gospel of Christ; for it is the power of God unto salvation to every one that believeth."

What lessons shall we draw from this theme appropriate to the hour? We know that Paul made no mistake. His Gospel did go to Rome and it did win. It captured the city and the empire; regenerated society from top to bottom. It ended polygamy and slavery. It tore down the amphitheatres and stopped the debasing gladiatorial shows. It saved for coming generations the civilization of the world. His Gospel was vital with Divine power.

The doctrines of the Fatherhood of God and the brotherhood of man, of actual sin and inherited depravity, of an ample atonement made for it by a Divine Savior, who justifies those who repent and believe, and the Holy Spirit who sanctifies those who receive the baptism with the Holy Ghost, and eternal retribution for those who will not be saved—these are truths that never can be eliminated and have any power left. They are as lasting as the love of God, as enduring as the needs of the soul. To try other means than these is to go back to instrumentalities that had utterly failed two thousand years ago. To attempt to lift the world by any other method is as futile as it would be to try to pry up Pike's Peak with a rye straw.

And this Gospel is not only *efficient*; it is *sufficient* even today. You may point me to the injustices of our times, to the labor-troubles, to communism, to the corruptions of our cities, the wickedness of Philadelphia, and Chicago, and New York; you may even cite me to the Pall Mall Gazette in modern London, and question the adequacy of the Gospel. But remember that even London, with all her reeking leprousy [*sic*] of guilt, is *white* compared with the moral blackness of that Rome to which Paul preached his Gospel.

Preach the full Gospel of justification for sinners, and sanctification and a life of holiness for believers. It would cure the selfishness and avarice and lust from which spring all our social troubles. Nothing more is needed than the real religion of Jesus, with men to preach it faithfully with the fervor of the great apostle, and such persons to help them as those men and women who labored with him in the Gospel. It can cleanse our cities, settle our labor difficulties, evangelize the nations, and conquer the world for Christ.

Lastly, we need not be ashamed of this religion of Jesus as a source of personal hope. The wonderful life Paul lived, he lived by faith in the Son of God. The love of Christ constrained him. It was his meat and drink to do the will of Jesus. For him to *live* was Christ. He knew no will, formed no plan, cherished no desire apart from his Lord. To him, Christ was the object of all longing, the reward of all toiling, the end of all hope. And when his hour came, he was ready to be offered up, knowing that to depart was to be forever with his Lord.

Only yesterday I stood by a poor widow, dying in poverty. When her eyes were closed to all earthly scenes and she no longer saw her human attendants, she stretched up her thin arms and said: "I am waiting, waiting, waiting for Jesus." Let us love this old Gospel, enshrine it more completely in our hearts, walk by it in life, pillow our heads upon it in death. We shall then sweep through the gates exclaiming: "I am not ashamed of the gospel of Christ; for it is the power of God unto salvation!"

Sermon IV
MOCKING AT SIN
"Fools make a mock at sin." Prov. xiv.9.

SIN IS THE VIRUS of spiritual beings, the moral malaria of God's universe. Its very existence is mysterious; its birth is unexplainable; its influence is subtle, and its results are awful in the extreme. What facile pen can picture it? What eloquent tongue, even though it be gifted like an angel's and blessed with all the powers possible to a finite intelligence, can fitly describe the evils it has wrought?

I. Let us notice some of the manifest effects of sin. We need not go far to find them. We live and walk, we wake and sleep in its evil influence as an atmosphere. Sin has somehow cast the shadow of its dire evils upon physical nature. The very ground is cursed for man's sake; the thorns and briers are reflections of his unworthiness. The wasting pestilence, the consuming drouth [*sic*], the swelling flood, the sweeping tornado, the destroying earthquake, the riving thunderbolt, are, through some mysterious affinity, sequences, as it were, of moral evils.

But these are only indirect and remote and comparatively harmless consequences of sin. For it lays hold upon man with a grasp of iron, though its least touch is a dire curse. The entire bodily organization is deranged by it. It puts its torturing fingers upon the sensitive nerves, and they writhe and throb with pain. Sin makes wounds and bruises and putrefying sores. It puts to the rack every sense, every member, every faculty of the human body, every organism, every muscle, every nerve. If it were possible to gather together and inspect at a single glance the awful aggregate of its purely physical effects, we should all be *appalled* at the heart-rending spectacle.

Suppose we could assemble, in one vast concourse of suffering, the pain-stricken, the diseased, the maimed, the lame, the halt, the blind, the distressed, the bleeding, the broken; could empty all hospitals and sick-rooms, and invalid chambers; could spread side by side all earth's convulsed death-beds; could swing the doors of its asylums and let the inmates be marshalled in one vast army of madness and driveling idiocy; could bring the anguished babes, the famine-pinched, the bereaved mothers, and all the bowed and wrinkled and infirm children of age; could unlock our dungeons and empty all our scaffolds, bring all suffering criminals and inebriates, the weary, the heartbroken, the passion-tossed, — bring every one from every quarter of the earth who has an ache or a burden or an infirmity or a disease or a wound occasioned by sin, to this common assemblage of woe! Great God! who but thee could bear the unutterable vision? What finite ear could endure the cries and groans and maniac shrieks and sobs and sighs and wails of this hideous, frightful chorus of physical woes which sin ever occasions?

But let not the march of our thought halt here. Let us move on with quickened energy to the consideration of the still greater and more deplorable effects of sin upon the soul. Outward evils are but the shadows of inward realities. If by some mighty effort of the imagination we could conceive; or if by some supernatural revelation we could know what is felt and done within the bosoms of men, the mind itself would be unhinged, and reason would flee from her throne in contemplation of it.

Could we but see, as God sees, all the fierce hatreds, the consuming lusts, the corrupting desires, the unappeased longings, the wasting griefs, the stingings of conscience, the stifling fears, the cruel disappointments, the raging jealousies, the burning revenges, the tortures of remorse, the goadings of anguish, the unutterable woes of despair that gnaw and torment and rack and consume hearts that still live to suffer on, unwasted and inconsumable;—could we thus see and know, as God does, what moral beings are suffering for one moment of time, the knowledge might utterly overwhelm and forever paralyze the onlooking. Nothing else could be thought of. The whole universe would appear to be one vast, rayless, shoreless ocean of woe, whose waves of suffering and agony roared louder than the thunder, and heaved and tossed without intermission forever.

But, friends, all this is just as real as though we, in our littleness, could *see* it and *know* it. Sin *has*, sin *does* this very moment wrap this world in a mantle of physical and mental anguish. How many other worlds are thus afflicted we know not. But here, at least, it inflicts every pain, wrings out every tear, burdens every breaking heart, wounds every tortured spirit, extorts every groan, convulses every death-bed, and digs every grave. Wherever it is, it will work a similar havoc. "Sin is a disease of the soul! a paralysis that weakens! a leprosy that pollutes! a plague that tortures! a pestilence that destroys!" a crime that damns every being within whose bosom it is permitted to dwell. Its only mission is destruction; its only possible wages is death; not physical death merely, but all that

that dread word means, — *the loss of Holiness, Happiness, and Heaven.*

There shall be, there are no tears, no crying, no pain, no death in Heaven, simply because no sin is permitted to enter that blessed realm.

But the shadow of sin even falls there; for God is there, and His loving heart must sadly miss the faces of the fallen sons of light who should ever be ministering in glory before His throne. And Jesus is there, bearing the print of the nails and the wound of the spear. Calvary cannot be forgotten. The incarnate God, whom sin assaulted with all its accursed agencies, working the ineffable iniquity of the crucifixion, can not forget that the same wickedness still exists, and every day spits upon Him and smites Him, crucifies Him afresh and puts Him to an open shame. Yes, the whole earth is tormented, and groans and travails under its burden of sin, and Heaven itself misses some of its brightness and glory because of it. Sin is the loss, the shame, the torment, the eternal detriment of the whole empire of God.

II. It is not difficult now to see why he is a fool who mocks at sin. In the common language of men, one is called a fool who acts as if not guided by good sense, nor possessed of ordinary intelligence and prudence. Plainly, then, he is acting the fool, who treats as of no consequence anything so disastrous, so powerful, and so far-reaching in its influence as sin. He is called *a fool* who wastes treasures or despises things precious, or mocks at danger, or defies destruction. It is *irrational*; it is *senseless*; it is playing *the fool.*

A famous queen of the Orient once dissolved a precious pearl and drank it in a cup of wine to the health of her guests; she was playing the fool. Once an Indian chief, intoxicated with vanity and a spirit of wreckless daring, and imagining that he could stem the mighty flood, pushed his bark canoe into the rapids and went over Niagara. A venturesome fool! A man that hides a viper in his bosom is a fool. A man who assaults an enraged lioness in a jungle when robbed of her whelps, alone and empty-handed, is a rash fool. But what of the man who mocks at sin? It is stronger than a lion; its sting is deadlier than any scorpion's; the fell sweep of its mighty tide of evil influences is more irresistible than a Niagara torrent, and with infernal chemistry it dissolves even the "pearl of great price" in the cup of its unhallowed indulgence. Make a mock at sin! As wise would it be to furnish your nursery with gun-cotton and dynamite for your children's playthings. As well would it be to take no precautions against cigars and matches, and nails in the boots, around a powder mill. A single grain of sand somehow worked its way into the granulating department of Laflin & Rand's powder factory in Paterson, N. J., on November 3, 1880. It was a little thing, only a trifle, but its friction caused the ignition of the powder, and a fearful explosion occurred, which destroyed the mill and blew the workmen into eternity. What a foolish thing to ignore such a possible result! But, ah me! men are found every day who are ready to make a mock at sin, whose least temptation may be a spark of fire to some unexpected magazine of passion whose fierce explosions will create eternal havoc in the soul. *Fools, fools! Inconsiderate fools!*

III. It remains for us to notice in what various ways men really do mock at sin; that is, make light of it as an unimportant thing. It may be we shall find that we have all been more or less guilty of playing the fool.

1. Those do it who openly boast of their sins, and who glory in their exploits of wickedness. How often have I seen a group of men talking together, glorying in their shame, each in turn laboring to prove himself viler than his fellows! Any day on our city streets you can hear men

boasting of deeds with a kind of diabolical pride, about which they ought to be silent and blush with unspeakable shame. St. Paul wept over the mob "whose glory is in their shame."

2. Those who smile on the sins of others and willingly profit by them, and thus lend tacit encouragement to evil doers, are mocking at sin. It is done in business by Christian men winking at the sins of wicked partners, and sharing in the profits of their knavery. It is done in society by Christian people knowingly putting themselves in intimate association with the vile enemies of Christ. It is done in politics when people adhere to their party, right or wrong, blind to its political crimes. It is done weekly, daily, almost hourly, and it is becoming one of the grave questions of an upright man how he can avoid it.

3. They are mocking at sin who ridicule its reprovers, and set themselves in wilful opposition to those who are seeking its reformation. God's reformers have nearly always been martyrs through public abuse and hate.

Wesley and Finney and Phillips and Garrison trod no easy path. They wore a crown of thorns before they wore a chaplet of flowers. Fighting against such men is often one and the same with fighting against God. Even when they are indiscreet and impractical, as reformers often are, still we must beware how we oppose them and impugn their motives, and ridicule their efforts, lest we be found to be defending the evils which they combat, and thus become of the number of those who mock at sin.

4. They especially mock at sin who knowingly and willingly set a bad and contagious example for others, and encourage them to continue in wrong doing.

It makes one shudder to think how much this is done. As to bad examples, how few do not set them! Number if you can the people who, by their neglect of the ordinances of God's house and by their irreligion, and their sneers at ministers and churches and the means of grace, are beguiling the young to walk in the counsel of the ungodly, and emboldening the old to sit in the seat of the scornful. All these are the unpaid emissaries of the prince of darkness, who spend their lives making a mock at sin.

5. Then there is that large class of people who, by their teaching and creed, hold out false hopes to the sinful. They lift their scornful outcry against the solemn warnings in Holy Writ of endless retribution, and laugh at the consequences of disobeying God. The air is full of it. It appears in the witticisms of the platform and the press, and in the coarse ribaldry of places of public resort.

The sublime utterances of the old prophets to deter men from iniquity, the solemn assurances of the apostles, the tender but still more terrible proclamations of the Son of God of an endless wrath upon final impenitence, are the passing jests of the street. It is practically a stifling of the voice of God to the soul, and a making sport of the pollutions and consequences of sin.

A plague once raged in ancient Athens. While the decaying bodies of the dead lay about the streets unburied, and multitudes were in mortal agony, and the very atmosphere was pregnant with death, the low and vile would gather in deserted palaces and abandon themselves to the most degrading excesses. The air was burdened by their blasphemies and the sound of their horrible revelry. Instead of supplicating the gods, they practiced their hideous orgies in the very face of death. So do men forsake the counsels, and despise the entreaties, and laugh at the threatened judgments of a holy God. They even stand on the brink of eternity, and face its darkness and deride its perils, and thus, like fools, make a mock at sin.

6. They commit this folly who, though not abandoned to profligacy of morals, still cling to sin and resist the pleadings of the Spirit, and procrastinate the day of repentance and salvation. It is no slight thing for one to deliberately resolve to continue a little longer

in disobedience and rebellion against God. It is no light thing for a soul to say, either by act or word, "O Lord, I want to have my own way a little longer, and follow a little farther the way of the transgressor; a little more of self-indulgence and wrong doing. I may repent some time, but not yet, Lord; not yet." Ah, what a mocking at sin such conduct is! What an insult is such trifling to God Almighty!

It matters not how beautiful the exterior conduct may be, nor how courtly and gracious are the manners; whether the personal demeanor be gentle or gross, the underlying principle of a sinner's life is precisely the same, —a spirit of rebellion against God, a treating sin as if it were a trifle. You who are as yet unreconciled to God, you may think yourself a lovely person, and not much of a sinner. May the God of mercy and grace undeceive you, and check such mocking while it is yet on your lips. Such unbelief is as fatal as any other. What difference does it make whether you are torn to pieces by wild beasts in an amphitheater, or are poisoned by the genial odor of flowers, if, in either case, death is alike certain?

If you reject the offered mercy of God and wilfully postpone your day of repentance, you are making light of transgression, and mocking at sin. Though you in manners be gentle and your tastes refined, and your sensibilities tender, and your heart affectionate, yet, if God is not loved, and sin is not forsaken, and Christ is not accepted, you are still trifling with evil, and in covert rebellion against a holy God.

Your destroyer understands you. His enticements will all come in pleasing form— like the viper that stung Cleopatra to death, its breath mingled with sweetest perfume and covered over with flowers—but still destruction, with its unsightliness and horrors, is in them.

Though Satan come with smiles and honeyed speech, robed as an angel of light, he is still only Satan, his bosom glowing with infernal malignity, and his heart full of hellish wiles.

Oh, that I had the power to create in the minds of all perfect hatred of sin! In God's name I pray you, who read these lines, to cease mocking at it. Avoid these innocent-looking *beginnings* of evil; these so-called harmless indulgences and sweetened pleasures of sin. Shut your eyes and your ears, bar all the doors of your immortal spirit against the solicitations of evil. Its continued presence is contamination; its touch is leprosy; its vile embrace is certain death.

7. They mock at sin who talk of it *as a necessity*, and sneer at the possibility of holiness, and make light of God's commands to be holy. This is to set at naught the intercessory prayer of Jesus, and all His precepts, exhortations, promises, and expressed will that we should be sanctified. This is to scorn the tears and agony of Jesus who, *"that He might sanctify the people,* suffered without the gate."* This is to pour contempt on the precious blood of the Son of God, which "cleanseth us from all sin." Oh, how daring to smile upon carnality, the fertile mother of all sin, and spurn the baptism with the Holy Ghost, its only cure! Remember, you have in your very natures a moral atmosphere which can be aroused by temptation into a very simoon[1] of passion which will sear and blast the soul with its poisonous breath.

Cease, then, to sport with evil, or to mock at actual or inbred sin. Beware of all temptations! Look not upon the wine-cup! Its odor is fragrant; its taste is sweet; it is beautiful to look upon; but delirium and death are in its ruby depths.

Beware of evil books! Many of them corruscate with flashes of genius. Alas! that "imperial lepers" should go forth from "palaces of thought" to scatter seeds of iniquity in the minds of the young, that shall wave in an immortal harvest of destruction.

Beware of lewd and profane and Sabbath-breaking and infidel companions. "Evil communications corrupt good manners." The wicked will receive you into their companionship, sensitive and pure and reverent and true; they will soil your modesty, dull your conscientiousness, chill your reverence, trample upon your virtues, and start you on a path of evil-doing, along which you will hasten "as if enamored of damnation"!

Oh, may God teach all our hearts the solemn lesson! Sin, like the carnality which mothers it, has in it despair and destruction and death and Hell. Hate sin, and flee from it for your very life.

But, O soul! sin is *in* you; by nature you are depraved and in bondage to it. Flee, then, to your atoning Savior, who can forgive you, and welcome the Holy Spirit, who can cleanse you, and break the galling chains of its terrible bondage.

Throw open every avenue of your being, and welcome God to come in and save and sanctify, and give eternal deliverance. *Oh, what an unspeakable fool is he who rejects such a salvation, and makes a mock at sin!*

Note

1. A *simoon* (Arabic, *simoom*) is a very hot, dry windstorm of sand. —*Ed. 2017*

Sermon V
A Savor of Life Unto Life, or of Death Unto Death

2 Cor. ii.14-16.

Paul drew his imagery from the well known customs of his time. We have an example in that striking passage in 2 Cor. ii. 14-16: "Now thanks be unto God, which always causeth us to triumph in Christ, and maketh manifest the savor of his knowledge by us in every place. For we are unto God a sweet savor of Christ, in them that are saved, and in them that perish: to the one we are the savor of death unto death; and to the other the savor of life unto life. And who is sufficient for these things?"

The "triumph" in Christ, always accorded to faithful ministers, has reference to the triumphal procession conferred upon a victorious general on his return from a successful war, in which he was allowed a magnificent entrance into the capital. In these triumphs the victorious commander was usually preceded or attended by the spoils of war, and by the princes, nobles, generals or people whom he had subdued. When Pompey was accorded his triumph, his chariot was drawn into the city by elephants. For two days the grand procession of trophies from every land, and a long retinue of captives, moved into the city along the *Via Sacra*. Brazen tablets were carried, on which were engraved the names of the conquered nations, including one thousand castles and nine hundred cities.

The word "savor" is used to denote a pleasant or fragrant odor as of incense or aromatics. There is an allusion here to the fact that in the triumphal processions fragrant odors were diffused, flowers of grateful smell being scattered in the way. On the altars of the gods incense was burned and sacrifices offered, and the whole city was filled with the fragrant smoke and with delightful perfumes.

So the apostle speaks of the savor of the knowledge of Christ. In Paul's triumphal career the knowledge of the Redeemer was diffused, like the odors in the triumphal march of the conquerors. And that odor was acceptable to God, as the fragrance of the incense was pleasant in the march of the returning victor. The effect of the apostle's teaching was to make Jesus known and the principles of His kingdom declared. It pleased God to have His redemptive grace proclaimed, even though there were many who might not avail themselves of it and would accordingly perish.

In these words of the apostle there is much both to encourage and to solemnize our hearts.

I. The true minister of the Gospel, with the Spirit of God in his heart, is a mighty power in the world. Lucius Mummius, the Roman consul, conquered all Achaia, and destroyed Corinth, Thebes and Colchis, and by order of the Roman Senate was favored with a triumph and was surnamed Achaicus.

But when Paul entered that same country a poor, footsore, weary, unattended preacher of the Gospel, he was a mightier conqueror than Mummius. Men did him the honor to declare that he was one of those that turned the world upside down. Mummius did nothing but slay and destroy, pillage and burn. His work was wholly *de*structive. Paul's work was *con*structive. He started influences that renovated the inner life of the people—influences that are felt there today, and will be as lasting as time.

Hannibal, one of the mightiest of all earthly conquerors, came with his legions to the gates of Rome, and all but took the city.

Paul entered the city as a prisoner in chains; but with the resistless "Sword of the Spirit"—the Gospel of Christ, he and the preachers that came after him captured the city and the throne and the legions and all the provinces of the mighty empire; and their influence is felt where Roman legions were never seen. Not a fragment of the great empire is left; but the influence of those preachers is in the full vigor of an immortal prime, marching on, conquering and to conquer the entire world.

Julius Caesar was, by common consent, the greatest pagan of the ancient world. He invaded Britain. Nothing is left of that invasion but a few stones underground here and there that mark the fortifications of his camps. But the Christian missionaries that followed him a few centuries later and entered the island without pomp or splendor or banners or armies, with only the Gospel of peace in their hands and the love of men and of God in their hearts, laid the foundations of institutions that stand there today, in their vast and far-reaching beneficence, like a "tree of life" to the nations.

Alexander the Great marched to India and covered some battlefields with the slain; but the names of Martyn and Judson and Scudder and Thoburn outshine all the bejewelled kings and princes and conquering warriors of India.

The warriors of Babylon and Syria and Rome and

France and England, have successively overrun Africa; but the lustre of Moffat and Livingstone and Taylor can never be obscured.

England sent the flower of her army over to America to fight her colonies. She has since sent her royal princes and titled statesmen to our shores; but she gave us her greatest treasures when, with the rude hand of persecution, she flung to us the godly pilgrim and Puritan ministers and the noble Scotch Presbyterians who built on the Rock Christ Jesus the foundation of this Christian republic. It is President Elliot, of Harvard, who says he would rather be the minister who founded Harvard College than to be any president this republic has had since the first. Oh, it is a wonderful thing to be counted worthy to preach the Gospel, to be put in trust with this mighty message of life that touches the very springs of spiritual activity and awakes powers and influences that never cease to be felt. It may seem to some that preaching is a simple and unworthy calling; nevertheless it has pleased God by the foolishness of preaching to save men, to build up His kingdom in human hearts—the only enduring thing in the world. Paul felt it. He magnified his office. He thanked God for it. He felt that he was given a victory over the wickedness of the earth, over the enemies of the Gospel; he was given success in planting the kingdom of Christ in human hearts. He was marching on under the approving eye of Jesus and the unseen hosts, with more solid and substantial joy in his soul than was ever felt by a Roman general returning from his conquests, laden with the spoils of victory, and attended by humbled princes and kings in chains, when assembled thousands shouted "*Io triumphe!*"

II. We are assured by this Scripture that the work of an honest and faithful ministry is especially pleasing to God. "For we are unto God a sweet savor of Christ in them that are saved and in them that perish." Like the smell of pleasant incense to men were the consecrated labors and ardent zeal of the faithful ambassadors of Christ to God. And this was true irrespective of their apparent success. They were responsible only for fidelity to the message, to the Master who sent them, and to the hearts of men. Whether men were saved or lost, whether the preacher had a nation at his feet like Samuel, or stood alone like Elijah; whether he was honored like Daniel, or cast into the dungeon like Jeremiah, or martyred like Isaiah, in any event God's mercy was proclaimed, His love made known, and his moral government over sinners justified. The honest ministers who cast in their lot with God, and help to make known the glories of His redemptive work to dying men, are accepted as a sweet savor, whether men persist in dying or not. God is still *true*, and His Gospel is *true*, and He is pleased with *it* and those who faithfully publish it to the world forevermore.

III. We are taught that the Gospel and the ministry are twofold in their influence and operation. They are both a savor of "life unto life" and "of death unto death" to men. In other words, they bring salvation or hasten and deepen the damnation of all who hear. The purpose of the Gospel is to save *all*. It reveals provisions of mercy for all. If it does not reach all, if some reject and turn away in scorn and contempt, they necessarily incur a greater disaster and plunge to a darker doom.

The mind shrinks from the contemplation of so solemn a truth. One is loath to believe that the fate of the persistently wicked is more dire, and their everlasting woe is intensified by a Savior's dying for them, and by the proclamation of mercy to their guilty souls; but we cannot avoid this conclusion, however dreadful to contemplate it may be. It must be so in the very nature of things. The very *quality* of the Gospel that makes life, produces death. The self-same feature that makes *blessing* possible makes *woe* equally possible. All analogy teaches it. Startling as it may seem, we cannot deny it if we would. The thoughtful mind finds endless illustration of this principle both in the realm of matter and of mind.

Water is a liquid that moves easily upon itself. This fact adds immeasurably to its utility. It flows in streams and rivers, and becomes a mechanical power to men. It buoys up the navies of the world, and yet lets the swift coursers of the deep sweep through its tides at wonderful speed. It moves so easily that the slightest breath of air stirs it, and it keeps pure by perpetual motion. But this very quality that makes it so essential a blessing to man, also enables it to respond to the touch of the hurricane and lift its hoary waves to the sky, and toss the largest ships as so many chips on its billows, and hurl them with the shock of an earthquake upon the rocks, and burst dams and carry everywhere desolation and death.

The expansive power of steam enables it to drive our trains and run the levers and wheels and spindles of our factories, and to do the work of more than a billion of laboring men. But this same quality also enables it to blow up our boilers and hurl multitudes to sudden death.

Fire as a physical servant of man is a thousand times more helpful than steam. He who discovered how to produce it by artificial means, was by far the most beneficent discoverer the race can ever know. However, the same power that enables fire to feed upon fuel and heat water and fuse metals and cook our food and warm our homes, also enables it to consume our dwellings and lay our cities in ashes.

The quality which enables electricity to light our cities and move our cars and turn our engines and flash our thoughts around the world, also causes it to kill the poor lineman and rive our dwellings with the thunderbolt.

When we leave the material realm and view the nature of man, we find along the whole range of his faculties the same double possibility of blessedness and woe. The stom-

ach that can enjoy food can suffer hunger.
The nerves that can thrill with pleasure can throb with
pain. The refined taste that can appreciate the beautiful
in art and nature is perpetually tortured by the ugly and
the unsightly. The ear that is sensitive to tone and keenly
observant of every delicate modulation of sound, and able
to drink in ecstatic delight from rich harmonies of music
is tortured by the harsh, shrill, discordant tones that pierce
it perpetually.

The refined and tender sensibilities that fit a man to
receive transcendent joys from human friendship and
society, also rend his very soul with anguish over the
treachery of friends and the cruel heartlessness of man.

That freedom of the will, that self-sovereignty and self-
control which give a man the possibility of character and
manhood, and make him godlike and fit for Heaven, also
enable him to be depraved and sinful and devilish and a
child of Hell. Over against every Gerizim of earth there
is an Ebal. Pleasure and pain, blessing and woe, life and
death seem to be essential and inseparable attendants of
each other throughout the empire of God.

Let us not, then, turn away from this truth that the
faithful ministry of the Gospel brings life to some and
death to others. Solemn and awful though it be, it is analo-
gous with God's truth everywhere. To deny it is to blur
our spiritual perception and do violence to our mental
and moral being.

We are compelled, then, to face the awful fact that the
very preaching of God's blood-bought salvation is going
to hasten the ruin of some who hear. The *aim* is to save
men. The object of all the zeal and sacrifice and toil and
prayer is to bring men into reconciliation to God. The
tendency of the Gospel is to save men. For that purpose it
was devised with all the skill of an all-wise God. There is
sufficiency in the Gospel for all men, and it is as really
fitted to save one as another. However it may be received,

it is always in itself the same pure and glorious system of truth, full of benevolence and mercy. Its bitterest enemy cannot point to one of its provisions that is adapted or designed to destroy men, or make them miserable. All its powers and influences are those which are fitted to save. Even though it is the means of death to men, yet the Gospel is what it is in itself—a pure and holy and benevolent gift of a benevolent God.

To use the beautiful language of Theodoret: "We indeed bear the sweet odor of Christ's Gospel to *all*; but all who hear it do not experience its saving effects. Thus to diseased eyes even the light of Heaven is noxious; yet the sun does not bring the injury. And to those who are in a fever honey is bitter, yet it is sweet nevertheless. Vultures, too, it is said, fly from sweet odors of myrrh; yet myrrh is myrrh, though the vultures avoid it. Thus if some be saved, though others perish, the Gospel retains it own virtue, though some disbelieve and abuse it, and die."

Serious, awful truth! The minister gives himself to the most blessed of all possible Christian service. His heart's desire and prayer to God is that men may be saved. He goes to homes of trouble and sorrow and offers Gospel consolation. He goes to hearts of sin and tells of a reconciling Savior; to believers, and tells them of the sanctifying baptism with the Holy Spirit. The reception his message receives makes him the savor of life unto life or of death unto death.

The principle is this:—truth resisted deadens the soul. Hearts that do not break under the hammer of the Gospel grow harder than the nether millstone. The sensibilities that are not melted by the story of Calvary are frozen into obdurate impenitence. The will that does not bow to the motives of the cross grows gigantic in its mighty rebellion against infinite love. The mind that will not be enlightened by the streaming radiance of an atoning Savior will become impenetrable dark in its wilful blindness.

The believers that will not enter the Canaan of sanctification when it is offered them, turn back into the wilderness to die.

By every principle of moral and spiritual gravitation the man that falls from the highest pinnacle of exalted Christian privilege falls to the deepest abyss of guilt and woe.

This is a startling echo of the words of the Son of God: "Woe unto thee, Bethsaida! For if the mighty works which were done in you, had been done in Tyre and Sidon, they would have repented long ago in sackcloth and ashes. And thou, Capernaum, which art exalted to heaven, shall be brought down to hell... It shall be more tolerable for the land of Sodom in the day of judgment, than for thee."

IV. It still remains for me to consider for a moment the solemn responsibility which this truth lays upon us all.

1. To those of us who are, or ever expect to be, ministers or religious teachers. Paul felt it, and he cried out: "To the one we are a savor of life unto life, and to the other a savor of death unto death, and who is sufficient for these things?" For the arduous and responsible work of the ministry, for a work whose influence must be felt either in the eternal salvation or damnation of the soul, who indeed is sufficient? Who is worthy of so important a charge? Who can undertake it without feeling in himself unfit for it, and that he needs constant Divine grace? A faithful Scotch minister always had a plaid robe lying on the foot of his bed that he might rise in the night and wrap himself in it and pray for his people. One cold winter night his wife chided him for thus exposing his health. He exclaimed, "Oh, woman! I have six hundred souls to give account for at the day of judgment, and I know not how it is with some of them. I must needs rise and pray for them." John Bunyan, preaching one day, said to his people, "When you have your conscience sprinkled with the blood of Christ, when you have an entrance into the

holiest and have liberty in prayer *remember me.*" Dr. Alexander Maclaren said to his congregation: "Remember, I have a great work on hand, a great deal upon my conscience. Pray for me brethren, pray."

O, ambassadors of Christ! preach the full Gospel of salvation, the whole counsel of God—justification, adoption, sanctification and a life of holiness, ever crying, "Who is sufficient for these things?"

2. A word of warning to those who fill the pews and listen to the Gospel. The better the preaching is, and the more truth you receive, unless improved, the more perilous it becomes. By the solemnities of this theme God says to you, "Take heed how ye hear! how you treat the Gospel! what use you make of Christian privileges." Better be born in heathendom and live in utter ignorance of a Savior than to live in a community like this and know Him and reject Him! Better attend the most Christless university in all this land, where teachers are unbelievers and irreligion is rampant, than to attend this Holiness college and be taught by these reverent Christian professors, and leave these halls of learning a hardened rebel against God!

Better listen to the most heaven-defying infidel every Sabbath than to hear the faithful offers of the Gospel of full salvation only to turn from them with scorn. O, the dark fate of that wretched soul who is born of Christian parents, and reared at a family altar, and brought up in a Christian church, and instructed by a serious Christian ministry, and watched over and taught by Christian professors, only at last to despise it all and stagger out into a Christless career!

It is an awful transition to go from the blazing light of holiness into the endless night of outer darkness! O God, teach us! teach us all how to hear the Gospel: how to make a right use of Christian privileges: for "Who is sufficient for these things?"

Sermon VI
THE PERSONAL ELEMENT OF RELIGION
Rom. xii.6; Matt. xxv.15; 1 Tim. iv.14.

P ARTS OF THREE VERSES of Scripture put together make remarkable reading, and teach us impressive lessons much needed by us all.

Here they are:

Rom. xii. 6. "Having gifts differing according to the grace that was given to us."

Matt. xxv. 15. "To every man according to his several ability."

1 Tim. iv. 14. "Neglect not the gift that is in thee."

It is said that America's illustrious statesman, Daniel Webster, was once asked at a dinner table, "What is the most important thought that ever occupied your mind?" He answered in all seriousness, "The most important thought that ever entered my mind was the thought of my individual responsibility to God." He enlarged on that thought for some minutes in matchless eloquence, while great men listened with astonishment in solemn silence, and then he appropriately arose and left the room as if to be alone with his God.

It is this sense of personal responsibility to God, and

the expression of it toward men to which I wish to call the attention of my readers. There is a manifest want of individualism in church life and Christian activity, from which the kingdom of God is suffering great detriment. The trend of our time is toward clubs, corporations, lodges, fraternities, unions, organizations, companies, trusts, associations, and congregations; the *individual* is losing his identity, is wasting, is actually dying of self-neglect.

I write these words in the cheering hope that some readers may be aroused to self-consciousness and a sense of their personal obligations to men and to God. To this end I make the following observations:

1. God intentionally makes men to differ. He bestows on each a personality and an individuality all his own. Human beings destined for immortality are not made as bullets are run in a mold, all alike, to fill the same place, to do the same service, and to be used indiscriminately. We differ alike in natural endowments and in spiritual gifts. Each has his own peculiar form, features, tastes, inclinations, strength of will, balance of faculties, combination of powers and weaknesses, which make him peculiarly himself, unlike anyone else that ever did live, does live, or ever will live.

And we differ no less in our circumstances. No two souls move through life having precisely the same environment. Parentage, time of birth, domestic and social conditions, helps, hindrances, fortunes and misfortunes all more or less vary, sufficiently, at least, to give to the jewel of every life a setting all its own.

And likewise we differ in opportunities. God says to every soul, "Behold, I have set before *thee* an open door." No two have the same path lying before them, the same possibilities, the same successes and triumphs. Each soul has its own circle of influence as each star has its own separate orbit. To each his work is like the law of nature and of grace. A dew-drop has not the mission of a diamond. A lily-bulb has not the opportunity of an acorn. One is to produce a fragrant flower; the other is to grow into a forest monarch. So before the advancing feet of every soul, there opens an avenue of possible usefulness accessible to him alone.

2. I observe that as an ultimate fact, God knows us and deals with us as *individuals*. If He is to destroy an antediluvian world it is because each of the mighty mass has corrupted his way before God, and He prepares an ark for the saving of eight souls because they are individually righteous. If He sends the consuming flames of His wrath to devour Sodom, He does not forget to send His angels to deliver righteous Lot. If He decrees the doom of Jericho, He remembers the one woman of faith living upon the wall.

If He commissions the armies of Titus to destroy Jerusalem and annihilate a guilty nation, He tells His few believing children to escape to the mountains. "Ye shall be gathered one by one, O ye children of Israel," says God; "There shall be joy in the presence of the angels of God over one sinner that repenteth." This is God's way. His care is minute and particular. He knows all the secrets of each heart. He numbers the hairs of each head. He tasted death for every man. He offers Himself as a personal friend and Savior to each soul.

Luther used, it is said, to thank God for those little words, "my," "thee," "thou," "thy," "me," which are scattered so profusely through the Scriptures. "The Lord is *my* rock," "*my* fortress," "*my* deliverer." "When *thou* passest through the waters I will be with *thee*." "*Thou* shalt guide *me* with thy counsel, and afterward receive *me* to glory."

These all show God's estimate of the importance of the distinct personality of man. Apart from all others he is born. Singly and for himself he is held accountable to God. He is to repent for *himself*, believe for *himself*, live by *himself,* die by *himself,* and finally be judged by *himself* and stand or fall as an individual at the bar of God.

III. As might be expected from the foregoing, God rightly expects special service of each. Each flower has its own fragrance to shed, each star its own attraction to exert—its own light to emit; and each drop of water its own mission to fulfill. As Dr. Bushnell has wisely written: "If there were any smallest star in Heaven that had no place to fill, that oversight would beget a disturbance which no Leverier could compute; because it would be a real and eternal, and not merely a casual or apparent disorder. One grain of sand, more or less, would disturb or even fatally disorder the whole scheme of the heavenly motions. So nicely balanced and so carefully hung are the worlds, that even the grains of their dust are counted, and their places adjusted to a corresponding nicety. There is nothing included in the gross or total sum that could be dispensed with. The same is true with regard to the forces that are apparently irregular. Every particle of air is moved by laws of as great precision as the laws of the heavenly bodies, or, indeed, by the same laws; keeping its appointed place and serving its appointed use. Every odor exhales in the nicest conformity with its appointed place and law.

"Even the viewless and mysterious heat, stealing through the dark centers and impenetrable depths of the world, obeys its uses with unfaltering exactness, dissolving never so much as an atom that was not to be dissolved.

"What now shall we say of man, appearing as it were, in the great circle of uses? They are all adjusted for him: has *he,* then, no ends adjusted for himself? Noblest of all creatures and closest to God, as he certainly is, are we to say that his Creator has no definite thoughts concerning him, no place prepared for him to fill, no uses for him to serve, which are the reason for his existence?

"There is, then, I conclude, a definite and proper end or issue for every man's existence… Every human soul has a complete and perfect plan, cherished for it in the heart of God — a Divine biography marked out which it enters into life to live."

We may conclude, then, that God has laid upon each special duties, commensurate with his individual gifts and opportunities. There is a post of duty for every man in the army of the Lord, which he alone can fill, and which he has no right to abandon; nay, *cannot* abandon to another. The corporal cannot be the colonel, and the general cannot be a private. One must stand on guard and do picket duty; another must plan the campaign, and issue the orders and lead the hosts to battle. "As we have many members in one body, and all members have not the same office, so we, who are many, are one body in Christ, and severally members one of another." "And having gifts differing according to the grace that was given to us, whether prophesy, let us prophesy according to the proportion of our faith; or ministry, let us give ourselves to our ministering; or he that teacheth to his teaching; or he that exhorteth to his exhorting; he that giveth let him do it with liberality; he that ruleth with diligence."

The rich man cannot pray or repent by proxy, nor can he delegate to others the duty of giving. He that is called to rule must not neglect his ruling, and sigh for the place of the teacher or prophet. As well might the foot abandon the duty of walking — and clamor for the duties of the eye, or the ear, or the tongue. A duty to every man according to his several ability, and no provision for idlers, is the law of the kingdom of grace. A personal service, a personal effort, a personal obligation that is measured by no other man's degree of efficiency or endeavor; but only by God's gift and the Heaven-sent opportunity, is the first requirement of our Lord. Such is the *individualism of duty*, the *per-*

sonal element which constitutes a fixed principle in the kingdom of Christ.

And corresponding with these special duties are *special responsibilities*. The eye has the ability to see and is responsible for seeing; the ear has the ability to hear and is responsible for hearing; the feet have the ability to walk and are responsible for locomotion. These several responsibilities can by no possibility be changed. They rest where they do in the very nature of things. The superintendent of a railroad has his individual responsibility; the train dispatcher has his; the brakeman has his; the switch-tender has his. The position of each lays upon him his special responsibility for the safety of the traveling public; he has a distinct commission to do a distinct thing. So long as the duties of the position are assumed, the attending responsibilities can never be transferred to any other human being.

And so it is in the kingdom of God. We are each called, by a discriminating, electing grace to do an especial work, which nobody else can do, and which, if neglected by any one of us, will be forever undone; and the terrible responsibility for the failure will forever darken the guilty soul.

We are witnesses for Christ, each with his own personal testimony to give in the court of the world. We were converted one at a time; and to each of us was given the charge, "Let him that heareth say, Come!" You notice it reads, "Let *him* say," let each one *personally* take up and send along down through the ages the blessed invitation to "come" and "take of the water of life freely."

And to encourage this individual effort and develop this sense of personal duty and responsibility, God has given promises of individual reward. Not *the church* that converteth a sinner, but "*he* that converteth a sinner from the error of his ways shall save a soul from death." It is not written the *company* that goeth forth with weeping, but "*he* that goeth forth with weeping, bearing precious seed, shall doubtless return, bringing his sheaves with him." And at the last it will not be said, "Well done, thou good and faithful church and society," but, "Well done, thou good and faithful *servant*, enter thou into the joy of thy Lord." We are "the salt of the earth," each Christian being a grain having his own personal savor of holy, sanctifying influence to exert. We are "the light of the world," each individual being expected to reflect his own rays which the "Sun of Righteousness" has shed upon his soul, each person shining "as a light in the world."

What a solemn, awful responsibility rests upon every individual Christian to discharge his duty, to meet his obligation, to be faithful to his trust!

IV. Notice the abounding evidence that a proper sense of the individuality and personal responsibility of the unit in our church membership is sadly deficient. I might cite as the crowning evidence the feeble triumphs of our churches, the comparatively few conversions that are reported in our year books.

A single fact will suffice. A paper lies before me showing that the Methodist Episcopal churches of Iowa for four out of the last five years, with one hundred and forty-seven thousand members, had an annual net loss in membership, and the aggregate loss for five years is three hundred and seventy-eight. What could such a vast army of Methodists have been about? Were they taking a Rip Van Winkle sleep for five years? Let us devoutly hope it will not last twenty!

No honest mind can go to the Scriptures and read its prophecies and promises of Gospel triumphs and believe that such meager results are all that Christians have a right to expect from faithful effort. God's Word is not untrue. The Gospel has lost none of its power or fitness to move wicked hearts. The cross of Christ is not a waning power. We are compelled, then, to accept the alternative and conclude that the Gospel power is not applied, and due effort is not made to save men.

But the churches are running; the organizations are all manned; and at least, make a show of activity. Where lies the fault? I am forced to believe that there is an evil back of the organization and it is simply this, a lamentable deficiency of consecrated, prayerful, personal effort.

This is evidenced by the fact that the masses of men in immediate proximity to the churches are unrenewed, profane and recklessly godless. Christian truth is still the wisdom of God; the Spirit is still almighty to save; but the masses remain quiet and undisturbed, sleeping the sleep of death on the brink of Hell because no Spirit-filled individual goes to them personally and moves them by thundering alarms or tender persuasions to come to God.

Further evidence is also furnished in the painfully obvious want of Christian maturity and moral power in the majority of church members. God has made ample provision for the growing up of each believer out of weakness into the vigor of spiritual manhood, into great efficiency of Christian service. When we look for strength and maturity; the measure of the stature of the fullness of Christ, how often we find only infantile weakness. When we go to Christians seeking teachers, we find "they have need that one teach them again, and are become such as have need of milk and not of strong meat."

And why this want of growth and development? Simply because the powers of individual Christians have not been "exercised by reason of use"; because they have neglected the gifts that are in them, and have buried God-given talents in a napkin of sloth. Personal activity is a prime essential to personal growth in grace. The toilers become the strong men and women, the pillars of our churches. There are so many weak Christians because there are so many idle

Christians, so few grown Christians because so few working Christians.

Another evidence is found in the joylessness of Christian experience about which we hear not a little. There is opportunity enough for joy in Christ's service. There is joy and peace in the Holy Ghost. There is an unspeakable delight to be derived from the consciousness of being a co-laborer with Jesus in His great work of redeeming the world.

St. Paul, in the midst of his trials and hardships and persecutions and imprisonments, was "as sorrowful yet always rejoicing." His great soul knew the unutterable joy of saving men.

If the children of the King are lean-spirited and dyspeptic, it is because spiritual inactivity has made them diseased. If the sons and daughters of God walk amidst shadows instead of in the blessed sunlight of Heaven's conscious approval, if their lips are filled with wailings instead of hallelujahs, it is because they do not seek the empowering and put forth continuous, persevering effort to save souls. To travail in spirit until hearts are born again is to have one's own heart filled with transports of joy befitting the bosom of an angel. It is to have rich foretastes of Heaven.

Further evidence of this weak sense of personal responsibility is seen in parental neglect of the spiritual interests of children. From multiplying evidence of the most varied kind it is apparent that legions of believing parents do not make any personal application of Divine truth to the hearts of their children, do not lovingly and prayerfully teach them the Word of God, do not talk with them alone on the most sacred and vital of all subjects — their personal relation to Christ. And then these parents hope to compound with their consciences by sending their children to the Sabbath-school. As if they had any right to turn over to some other irresponsible person the religious training of the children which God has given to them to guide and prepare for Heaven.

When I was a student at Yale I was a member of the same church with the venerable ex-President Woolsey. He had two young daughters by a late marriage. He would not send them to the Sabbath-school, for he said God held him responsible for their training, and he spent a portion of Sunday afternoon teaching them.

Still more proof comes in the all too prevalent disposition to relegate to ministers the sole work of converting men. This is a vile relic of popery and one of Satan's most diabolical devices, this custom of regarding ministers as a class distinct from all others, to whom are entrusted all the concerns of religion. Perhaps unconsciously, but none the less really, many believers look upon the work of securing the conversion of men as a purely professional matter. As well might all the soldiers stand idly by and leave their generals to fight the battles! How utterly unlike the primitive church is this! Deacon Stephen and Deacon Philip were as anxious and laborious to secure the conversion of people as were the Apostles Peter and James, and there was a blessed band of yokefellows, men and women, who labored with the apostles in the Gospel. No doubt all the early believers understood that they were individually to do their utmost to multiply disciples for the Master, and this was as much the rule of life as it is now the exception. Today societies are somehow looked upon as substitutes for *persons; self* is lost in the congregation; the church is expected to be active while the individuals who compose it contentedly remain inactive; it is expected to gather in members whether the individuals gather any or not, as if the whole could be greater or do more than the aggregate of its parts.

And so it is that individualism is being crushed under ponderous organizations, and the precious disciples of the Lord are wasting innumerable opportunities, and are losing their sense of personal responsibility and all due conception of the calling of God and the grand end of life! Ah, how it delights Satan! Little does he care how vast the church is as a mass if only each individual member will sleep.

I will mention but one more sad indication of this evil. It is a common and well-nigh unchallenged saying that corporations have no souls. But pray tell, why not? They are composed of men, and men have souls. What is the real underlying reason but this, that the individual members of corporations, many of them Christians, have barricaded their consciences behind their business charters and have conveniently buried their honor and pity and justice and humanity in their articles of agreement. The corporation can now practice the grossest injustice, the most overreaching selfishness, and for the sake of gain can scout morals, drive men to the wall, drive hard bargains and grind their employees to the very dust. And if you go to each individual of the corporation and ask for explanation or redress, he will say: "Oh, it is too bad, quite too bad; but I am not responsible; the company did that!"

But, by and by, death will dissolve their soulless partnerships, and the *individuals* who composed them, standing at the bar of a holy God, will learn to their surprise and sorrow that somebody was responsible.

V. I would now call attention to some considerations which show the absolute necessity of more personal effort on the part of all who love Christ. Satan is terribly in earnest to curse the world. His followers are intensely and personally active. The drunkard is perpetually treating and soliciting companionship in his wickedness. The gambler will lay his snares and work for days and weeks and cross land and sea to rope in his victim. The licentious ply their hellish influence by day and by night, openly and secretly, and labor with all the tirelessness of a fiend to captivate, seduce and destroy. The skeptic, the infidel and the scoffer, are never backward to vaunt their hatred of religion, their opposition to Christ, and to scatter tracts and form societies, and loan books and to bear testimony against the truth. They boldly lift their ensign, and enthusiastically champion their cause. They are at it, and all at it, and always at it, seeking recruits to stand with them and hold aloft the black flag of rebellion against God Almighty.

Now, all this enthusiasm of wickedness must be met by a corresponding enthusiasm for righteousness. This zeal to destroy must be matched by zeal to save. This eager personal endeavor to lure souls to Hell must have pitted against it a similar personal endeavor to win souls for Christ and Heaven.

But this is only a partial statement of the case. The truth is that by no other possible means can the religious needs of the age be met. We have so much evil to contend with, so gigantic in its strength, so diffused in its influence, and so infectious and malignant in its effort that nothing short of the engagement, the energies, and the earnestness of the whole church can cope with it.

A single illustration will suffice. Twenty years ago I was a pastor in Allegheny, Pa. At that time, making the largest deductions needful for children too young to believe in Christ, there were one hundred thousand souls who, through choice, were without Christ and "without God in the world," and there were actually two hundred and twenty thousand souls in Pittsburg and Allegheny who were not indicated by the records as in any sense pious members and vitally connected with either Protestant or Catholic churches.

And to cope with the twenty-five hundred licensed saloons and all the aggregated wickedness which such cities represent, and to evangelize this vast population of more than two hundred thousand, there were all told only one hundred and fifty-five Protestant ministers.

It was apparent that though within easy reach of the open door of our sanctuaries, many scores of thousands avoided the ministers and the established means of grace. If such Christless masses in our cities ever hear the Gospel it must be carried to them by individual effort. But who must do it? The ministers? A single moment's consideration will make plain the impossibility of their doing it. No clerical force can be maintained that will be adequate for this stupendous work. Thousands of these people in the great cities are bitterly prejudiced against the clergy, which fact precludes their approaching them. Thousands upon thousands of these people are employed all day in shops and stores, and cannot then be seen; and the average city clergyman has church engagements four or five evenings in a week. Multitudes of these people sleep day times and work nights. A thousand obstacles intervene to prevent their being reached by a few professional men, whose hands are overloaded with work. No; the ordained ministry are utterly inadequate to meet this necessity. It was never designed by God that they should. He never intended that the ministry should do the whole work of the churches, and relieve the lay-membership of the duty to make personal exertion to save men. And the condition of human society will never be such that they *could* do it if they *would*.

Plainly this multitudinous work must be divided up among a multitude of workers. Each Christian must make an honest effort to build the wall of Zion over against his own house, to labor for the conversion of those under his own roof and in his own neighborhood. Each Sabbath school teacher must lay it upon his heart to do a portion of the work. The gentleman in the office must have a deep and abiding interest in the spiritual welfare of his clerks. The manufacturer must somehow give practical expression to a concern for the souls of his employees.

The Christian lady must have an eye to the cause of the Lord among her neighbors, and the Christian workman must live for Christ and talk for Christ among the companions of his toil. Each believer must feel that he has feet to run, and hands to work, and lips to speak, and a heart to love, and a mind to think and plan for Jesus; must realize that he is an ambassador for Christ with a commission sent from Heaven to *do* something and *be* something for that Savior who has done so much and been so much for him.

Oh, we surely need today Christians like Luke to write for Jesus, and Mary Magdalenes to run with swift feet and tell the sorrowing the glad news that their Lord has risen, and seamstresses like Dorcas and Prisca able to teach others "the more perfect way," and mechanics like Harlan Page, each bringing a hundred souls to Christ. We still need teachers like Mary Lyon and servants like Onesimus, and warm-hearted women like the Bible Marys to serve their Lord.

We still need men like Rufus and Lucius and Aquila and "Apelles, approved in Christ," and Christian sisters like Chloe and Tryphena and Tryphosa and "those women who labored with" Paul "in the Gospel." We sorely need a countless multitude of individuals who are always conscious of their individual responsibility to God, and who will not suffer their personality to be annihilated by church membership.

An English minister of fifty years ago, eminent for Christian usefulness, John Angell James, wrote on the very subject these burning words: "That is what we want. This we must have or we can never overtake the population of our country with the Gospel, and the means of grace. I say it again and again, and I say it with all possible emphasis, and would send it if I could with a trumpet blast over the land: *Societies must not be a substitute for per-*

sonal labors. Organization must not crush individualism... With all members of churches walking in holy conversation and godliness, sending forth the light of a beautiful example, full of zeal, laboring for the salvation of their fellows, and inspired with the ambition, and animated with the hope of saving souls by personal effort, each studying what he could do, and doing what he could, what might not be looked for as the glorious result of such general activity, zeal and earnestness?

What an awakening would take place, what revivals would come on! What prayers would ascend, and what showers of blessings would come down in their season!

"When our churches exhibit such scenes as these, then will God's work go on in the earth." And we may add, then, too, our progress will be with a speed hitherto unparalleled in human history.

VI. Let us consider briefly how this want in modern Christian life is to be met. First, evidently we are to feel it. This we will certainly do when we seriously, earnestly, prayerfully study the needs of Christ's kingdom. Our hearts will soon begin to ache with sympathy, and each will be prompted to cry, "Lord, what wilt thou have me to do?" And He would have you do *something* which is your special work. Spurgeon has well said: "There is not a spider hanging on the king's wall but hath its errand; there is not a nettle that groweth in the corner of the churchyard but hath its purpose; there is not a single insect fluttering in the breeze but accomplisheth some Divine decree; and I will never have it that God created any man, especially any Christian man, to be a blank, and to be a nothing. He made you for an end. Find out what that end is; find out your niche and fill it. If it be ever so little, if it is only to be a hewer of wood and a drawer of water, do something in the great battle for God and truth."

You will doubtless feel your unworthiness and be ready

to cry out, "O Lord, who is sufficient for these things?" This will drive, you to the mercy-seat for the oil of grace that your light may shine; for the holiness of heart that will give you a sanctifying influence; for the anointed lips and "the tongue of fire," that you may speak with an unction from the Holy One; and for a mind illuminated and taught by the Spirit that you may fitly hold forth the Word of life."

When you are thus moved and prayerful and in sympathy with the mission of Jesus, the means and the opportunities will open before you. When once your heart is alive with zeal and inflamed with a passion for souls, so that you will be impelled to determine, "I must do something to save souls; I must find means of doing good," you will be sure to find them. Your quickened mind will discern duties and detect needs; you will find some door of opportunity open, some needy soul for *you* to reach, some wayward spirit whom *you* can point to the Lamb of God.

VII. Lastly, consider what encouragements and motives incite us to personal work for Christ. Oh, if we could have just one worthy conception of our once crucified Lord of glory, we could never do enough for Him. We would be willing to imitate Paul, and entreat men night and day with tears to be reconciled to God.

Or, if we could have a faint appreciation of what it means to save one soul, what infinite anguish and degradation and woe it is saved *from*, and what endless growth in grace and inconceivable development in godlikeness, and eternal blessedness awaits it, our hearts would glow with the ardor of a seraph, and we could never be silent for pleading with men to be saved.

Or, again, if we could understand how disastrous mere negative piety may be to others it would make our hearts ache with grief over our past indolence, and we never again could be idle in God's vineyard. Would you stand

with folded arms by a railroad track on which some vil-
lain had placed an obstruction, meekly protesting your
innocence, while the express was sweeping down toward
it at fearful speed? Oh, how contemptible and culpable
would such do-nothing innocence be!

But, behold, the long, endless train of sin-laden humanity thundering along down to death! Have you no personal protest to make, no danger signal to lift, no warning to give? Shall none be entreated by you personally to
believe and live?

Consider, also, the principles of your faith. You believe
in a Divine Savior, who made an atonement for all the
race. You believe that it is God's will that all should be
saved from an endless Hell—and that, too, by human
instrumentality. You profess to believe all this, and dying
men and women around you know it. Fellow Christians,
we must either stop professing our belief in the stupendous realities of the eternal world, or we must act more
as if they were true. Personal zeal and godly living on
the part of Christians are the best possible antidotes for
popular infidelity.

Then consider what immeasurable and everlasting good
may result from personal endeavor. "Live today!" was
the morning salutation of John Wesley to Sophia Cook, a
young lady who lived in his house. Inspired by his words
she went out to live for Jesus, by teaching His Gospel to
children. She suggested to Robert Raikes the founding of
Sabbath schools and aided him, and that was the beginning of that institution that has brought such blessings
to the race.

Talmage once said: "It seemed to be a matter of little
importance that a woman, whose name has been forgotten, prayerfully dropped a tract in the way of a very bad
man by the name of Richard Baxter, and it was the means
of his salvation. In after days he wrote 'The Call to the
Unconverted,' which was the means of bringing a multi-

tude to God, among others Philip Doddridge. He wrote a book called 'The Rise and Progress of Religion in the Soul,' which has brought thousands to God, among others the great Wilberforce. Wilberforce wrote a book called 'A Practical View of Christianity,' which was the means of bringing multitudes to Christ, among others Leigh Richmond. Leigh Richmond wrote a tract which has been the means of the conversion of multitudes. And that stream of influence started from the fact that one Christian woman put a tract in the way of Richard Baxter—the great tide rolling on and on and on forever."

A half a century ago in Illinois, an audience was asked to do something for Christ. Little Mary Paxton began by asking her father to come to Sunday school. He was forty years old; could not read; hated Christians; but he loved his little Mary, and to please her came to Sunday school. He was converted and became the greatest Sunday school apostle of our land. He is said to have established 1500 Sunday schools with seventy thousand pupils from which sprang a hundred Christian churches. What a countless multitude that little child was starting to Heaven!

In Chicago, a woman asked a poor Swede to attend a religious meeting. She went and was converted, brought her husband and he was converted; and led the entire crew of a lake vessel to Christ. Moody told us of a precious revival in which he was, that was begun in the sick-chamber of a poor invalid who was flat on his back. He was distressed at the thought of the peril of sinners around him. He invited the brethren of the church to come to his chamber and pray for a revival; but they were too dead to pray. He invited the sisters; a few came and prayed and prayed till the Lord suddenly came to his temple with a wonderful blessing. Oh, who is too feeble, too sick, too poor, too young, or too old to do something for Jesus! Who can tell what the harvest will be of one personal endeavor to win a soul? Who can be willing to remain effortless and fruitless, to go home to Heaven alone and empty-handed, having no sheaves for the heavenly garner, to stand before Jesus like the barren fig-tree bearing nothing but leaves?

Oh, that all believers might apprehend that for which they have been apprehended by Christ Jesus! Oh, that they might know that they are each called to be a co-worker with Jesus in efforts to save a dying world! John Smith, a mighty Wesleyan preacher of a past generation, once wrote of himself, "God has given me such a sight of the value of precious souls, that I cannot live if souls are not saved. O, give me souls or else I die." If such a passion for soul-saving could take possession of every disciple of our Lord the world over, so that in the factory and warehouse and store and shop, in the field and by the way, at the fireside and in the social gathering, in the city and in the country, on the land and on the sea, men and women would be eagerly planning and watching for an opportunity to win someone for Christ, then compassion for the lost and perishing would burn in each heart, prayers for their salvation would ascend from each lip, and messages of love and mercy would be spoken by every tongue.

Then, O then, would tarry no longer the coming of the kingdom, and the redemption of our ruined race, Ye ransomed followers of Jesus, heed this call: consecrate yourselves to this work: begin at once to personally, persistently seek the salvation of some soul.

Sermon VII
WHAT IS MAN THAT
THOU ART MINDFUL OF HIM?

Psa. viii.3-4: "When I consider thy heavens, the work of thy fingers, the moon and the stars which thou hast ordained; What is man that thou art mindful of him? and the son of man that thou visitest him?"

THE STARRY HEAVENS HAVE ALWAYS called forth wonder and amazement from thoughtful minds. Every imaginative and reflecting soul is moved and thrilled by the sight of the splendor of the hosts of Heaven. David was no exception. When he lay on the Judean plains watching and guarding his sheep, he was moved by the sublimity of the night. He was led to exclaim. "When I consider thy heavens, the work of thy fingers, the moon and the stars which thou hast ordained; What is man, that thou art mindful of him? and the son of man that thou visitest him?"

About five thousand stars are visible to the eye. It seemed wonderful to the Psalmist that the exalted Being who fills the heavens and whom the Heaven of heavens cannot contain should waste a thought on such a creature as man. How much more wonderful would it have seemed to him if he had known some of the facts revealed by modern science. What if he had been told that this world, about which he knew so little; was twenty-five thousand miles around, and that it was whirling at the rate of a thousand miles an hour, and was shooting through space at the rate of nineteen miles a second, in comparison with which the swiftest cannon-ball is like motionless rest! What if he had been told that the sun was more than ninety million miles away, and was fourteen hundred times larger than our world! Suppose then that David had looked through a modern telescope that brings five million, five hundred thousand stars within the field of vision; and had been told that some of those stars were shining with five thousand times the magnitude and splendor of our sun, and are so far distant that light, traveling with the inconceivable speed of one hundred and ninety two thousand miles a second, is fourteen thousand years in reaching this little speck of a world. If David had known all these revelations of modern science, how much more would have been his amazement at the fact that God still condescends to notice man. "When I consider thy heavens, the work of thy fingers, the moon and stars which thou hast ordained; What is man, that thou are mindful of him? and the son of man that thou visitest him?"

I. Notice it is a fact that God is mindful of man very much so. Yea, He is more mindful of him that of all the glorious stars and suns that shine in all the firmament of God.

He has no concern for the stars, but He has the deepest concern over the fate of man. He never wept over burning suns, but He has wept over sinning and suffering man. He never expended any sympathy on the constellations, but the sorrows of men have awakened his deepest solicitude. He never visited a distant star to avert its fate, or alter its doom; but He did visit this far distant little planet to redeem man from destruction and visit him with the light and glory of a great salvation. He has proved to a certainty that He bestows more care and anxious love upon the humblest little babe in the poor man's cabin than upon all the material universe. "Thou madest him a little lower than the angels," but we may add, "Only a little." We have faculties in kind like theirs. We are hastening on to be their companions and to stand as peers among them. Yea, "know ye not that we shall judge angels?" There is a matchless career before us, a destiny bewilderingly glorious, a growth that will lift us in time above the stature and proportions of any angels now before the throne of God.

This is the stupendous truth at the bottom of the Holiness Movement. Man is too godlike in his origin, too glorious in his destiny, to waste himself in a career of sin. If he were only an animal, he might live as a beast lives on the low plain of animal indulgence. If he were a thinking machine merely clothed with flesh and blood, his fate would be a matter of no concern. But he is a child of God, made in the image of God, with a glorious destiny made possible to him, and crowned with glory and honor! What honor? The honor of the Son of God assuming his likeness. The additional honor also of the fact that Jesus, having picked up the poor, ruined, cast-aways of Satan, saves them, sanctifies them, and is then "not ashamed to call them brethren."

Surely so great a being as that ought to respect himself enough, and have sufficient regard for self-interest and the vast possibilities before him, to refrain from sin. Sin blights, sin destroys, sin damns. One sin hurled the angels out of Heaven! One sin shut our first parents out of Eden. One sin, unrepented of, and unforsaken, will shut any of us out of Heaven.

Holiness teachers, then, are on the right track. They hold up the heinousness of sin, and the glory and beauty of holiness; the measureless growth of a child of God, and his illimitable possibilities in eternal development; and they cry out to all with inspired emphasis, "Like as he which calleth you is holy, so be ye yourselves also holy in all manner of living; because it is written ye shall be holy; for I am holy."

II. We have seen that God has shown a marvelous and very peculiar interest in man. We have not adequately pointed out the reasons why. This we will now proceed to do.

1. Man is a criminal rebel against the government of God. It is surprising, when one stops to think of it, how a great crime fastens upon the criminal the interest and attention of mankind. There was recently a poor, mean criminal by the name of Tracey in a western prison, who was practically unknown to men. But he escaped and defied arrest, and, in fighting for his liberty, held at bay and evaded his pursuers for a month, killing in the meantime thirteen men. These foul and revolting crimes fastened upon him the attention of the whole nation, and he received more notice from the daily press than would be given to a hundred thousand quiet, law-abiding men.

The assassins of Lincoln, Garfield and McKinley were obscure enough before the commission of their crimes, but their dastardly deeds fastened upon them the attention of mankind and lifted them to an immortality of infamy.

A thousand ships can ply the peaceful traffic of the sea in quiet and obscurity, but let one of them lift the black flag of piracy and begin to wage war upon commerce, and at once this criminal ship elicits the attention of civilization. The description of this ship, her length, and shape, and color, and speed, and the number of her crew, become the common knowledge of mankind; and the navies of the nations will join their efforts to run her down.

Now, man is the rebel and the criminal of the moral universe. He has joined forces with Satan and the fallen angels in infernal assault upon the government and empire of God. As such, God and the moral universe bestow on him their attention, and concern themselves about his fate.

2. Man is sick. Well people receive comparatively little attention. The well children need but little notice. It is the inmate of the sick chamber that awakens anxiety and watchfulness, and about the invalid's couch or chair circles and swings the life of the home, and perhaps of the whole neighborhood. Now man is the sick member of the family of God. The angels of the skies, blessed with the perfect health of Heaven, bend above him and are all ministering spirits ready to serve. The Father's heart is touched with sympathy, and the Physician of Nazareth stands by in readiness to heal.

3. Man is lost. With what quiet uneventfulness the home life moves along in a blessed monotony for weeks and months and years. But let little Mary toddle off into the forest, wander among the crags and chasms of the mountain side, and at once what a sudden end of peace! What a consternation in the home and neighborhood! How are all peaceful employments abandoned while men and boys turn out and hunt night and day for the lost.

Is there nothing like this in the spiritual realm? What brought Jesus on His long missionary journey from the skies? Was it not to seek and to save the lost? The thirty-three years journey over the inhospitable plains of a Christ-rejecting, heaven-despising, holiness-hating world, through dark Gethsemane and over the ragged steep of Calvary, what was it all but a journey after the lost? And God and Heaven are still engaged in the diligent search after lost, fallen, sick and sinful men.

4. But man is also a sentient being, capable of joy or suffering, and that eternally. How wonderful does this fact lift our lives into great significance. Let any millionaire waste his millions in riotous and senseless prodigal-

ity, and no law will stop him—no hand be lifted to stay his folly. But let that same man turn around and go to torturing the meanest and most worthless cur that ever wakened slumber by barking at his shadow in the light of the moon, and at once he will be arrested for cruelty to animals. The dog has more significance in the eyes of the law than all his millions, because it can suffer.

Man, measured by such a standard, is of how great a significance! How much enjoyment is possible to him during the lapse of ages? Not an angel in Heaven could compute and answer the query. How much could he suffer in the cycles of a lost eternity? The mind reels in contemplation of the awful problem.

Let us illustrate it. All the vast waters of the Atlantic Ocean could be passed through an aperture not larger than a straw of wheat. Nothing is needed but an infinity of time to accomplish the surprising result. President Finney used to say that one lost soul during the sweep of eternity could suffer, and doubtless would suffer, more than all the universe has suffered up to the present time. Nothing but constant suffering and the eternal duration of a lost soul are needed to reach the appalling result. God, who made man capable of such an infinitude of joy or suffering, appreciates his importance. The whole physical universe dwindles into insignificance compared with one single soul capable of joy or suffering, and that forever.

5. Man is capable of endless development, either in godlikeness or the opposite. "It doth not yet appear what we shall be." None of us can ever dimly conjecture what eternal growth can make of any of us. Sir Isaac Newton was born so feeble a little babe, only a couple of spans long, that for days he hovered between two worlds, a mere flutter of life. But in forty years he was calculating the speed of that light to which his baby eyes so tardily opened, and was weighing planets and stars in the scales

of his mighty intellect! If a child can make such growth in less than half a century, what will an eternity of development do for the least of us?

Each lost sinner will some day be a more bloated and horrible monster of iniquity than Satan is now. And every redeemed saint finally saved will some day outshine in radiance, and be taller of stature, nobler in growth of godlikeness, than the mightiest archangel now blazing in glory before the throne of God.

Such reflections as these answer partially, at least, the question, "What is man that thou art mindful of him?" They lead us to stand in awe before the possible destiny of man.

Sin is too dangerous to fool with in view of the awful peril involved. Holiness is too inviting to be neglected in view of the reward —the infinite prize to be won. We reiterate once more the ringing words of God, "Like as he who hath called you is holy, so be ye holy in all manner of living. Ye shall be holy, for I am holy."

Sermon VIII
THE CLEANSING BAPTISM

Acts xv.8, 9, 11: "And God, which knoweth the heart, bare them witness, giving them the Holy Ghost, even as he did unto us; and he made no distinction between us and them, cleansing their hearts by faith… But we believe that we shall be saved through the grace of the Lord Jesus, in like manner as they."

PREJUDICE IS ONE OF THE SADDEST EVIDENCES that ours is a fallen race. It is so universal that it seems as if none escape. Individuals are so prejudiced against each other that they will not co-operate for a common good. A Luther refuses to have any fellowship with a holy Zwingle. Families are kept aloof from each other. Churches often times will have nothing to do with rival denominations. In some countries there is a proud and bitter caste-spirit utterly foreign to the Gospel. Prejudice separates nations, till they watch each other with envious eyes across a Rhine. Races treat each other as if they were children of a different God, with nothing in common. It took two visions from Heaven to get Peter and his Gentile audience together. The Jews felt an ill-disguised contempt for all the rest of mankind. To the intellectual Greeks all the rest of the world were ignoble Barbarians. The white race today has much the same feeling for the black races.

The saddest form of prejudice and the most harmful is that against TRUTH. It leads people to be inhospitable to any new revelation, or any new idea, or any advance in doctrine. It led the ancient Hebrews to reject Christianity. It keeps Mohammedans from doing it now. It led Roman Catholics to reject the light of the Reformation. It led Englishmen to persecute Wesley and reject the doctrine of the witness of the Spirit, and afterward to oppose him for advocating the doctrine of perfect love.

I beseech you to lay aside this prejudice. It is an imp direct from the bottomless pit. Do not think that your little denomination or school of thought has a corner on all truth. Keep an open eye for light from any quarter; stand four-square to all the winds of truth that blow. Banish from your heart at once and forever all unwillingness to hear about this Scriptural doctrine of sanctification. To oppose it is to oppose the Holy Spirit, who reveals it to our minds and brings the experience into our hearts.

In discussing the text observe,

I. God makes no difference. He "made no distinction between" Peter and his fellow-disciples, and Cornelius and his Roman soldiers. When it comes to appearing before God and pleading for mercy, no man living stands an inch above his fellows. Rich and poor are alike spiritual paupers. Educated and ignorant need alike the illumination of the heavenly Teacher. High and low alike need to be lifted from the pit of depravity and sin into which they have fallen. All are in condemnation, that God may have mercy upon all.

A prominent lawyer and his wife in New York City, weary of the senseless round of fashionable gayety, went to a city mission for a new kind of amusement. They were both church-members, having a form of godliness without the power of it. They sat on the platform and listened to the Gospel preached to the vile men and women from the slums. When the altar call was made the filthy, vermin-infested creatures rose from the audience and started for the altar. The brilliant lawyer and his fashionable wife rose on the platform, both under conviction, and also started for the altar. The leader in consternation tried to keep them back: but they said, "We want that Savior, too." And there they knelt, the cultured and proud and richly dressed, kneeling with the soaks, and bums and harlots at the same altar, and found the same Christ. That Christian lady was afterward sanctified and is now managing one of the most effective homes for the fallen in New York City. God, when she was seeking mercy, put no difference between her and the woman of the street.

McNeil, of Scotland, was preaching a sermon from the text: "For there is no difference." At the close an aristocratic lady came up to him and asked: "Did you say there is no difference?" "Yes, ma'am, God says it." "Must I be saved just like my coachman, John?" "Yes, ma'am, if you are saved at all, you must be saved just like your coachman." "Then I won't have it at all." And away she went in a pet of indignation, taking a straight course to the pit. The same kind of pride sends multitudes to Hell. All the accidents of life, race and color and rank and station, are nothing to God in matters of salvation. There is no difference; "all have sinned and come short of the glory of God."

II. The text informs us that God knoweth all hearts. Nobody else does. We cannot tell the true condition of the heart of our most intimate friend. We may be a stranger to the one that lies in our bosom. Even inspired Samuel could not see the want of kingship in the eldest born of Jesse. God had to tell him, "Man seeth not as God seeth: for man looketh on the outward appearance, but, God looketh on the heart." Neither his father nor his brothers knew the kingly soul of David; but he was known to God.

We often do not know our own hearts. The old prophet said: "The heart is deceitful above all things and desperately wicked: who can know it?" God let Elisha have a view of Hazael's heart, and the prophet began to weep. "And Hazael said, Why weepeth my Lord? And he answered, Because I know the evil that thou wilt do unto the children of Israel: their strongholds wilt thou set on fire, and their young men wilt thou slay with the sword, and wilt dash their children, and rip up their women with child." And Hazael said, "But what, is thy servant a dog that he should do this great thing?" He could not believe that he could ever be guilty of such atrocities; but he lived to do them. He simply did not know his own heart, and its awful capabilities of wickedness.

But God is never deceived. He knows the sinner's heart—its malignant depravity, its awful depth of corruption, its open hostility against God and righteousness, and its bent to sin. He knows a *penitent*, and "a broken and contrite heart" He will not despise. He knows and loves a *justified* heart, and sends the Spirit of adoption to lead it to cry "Abba Father." Men deny that there are any sanctified hearts: but God knows them. "The eyes of the Lord run to and fro throughout the whole earth to show himself strong in behalf of them whose heart is perfect toward him."

III. The text declares, "God bare them witness." This is the peculiar work of the Holy Spirit, to bear witness to every person of the condition of his heart. Jesus said, "When he is come he will convince the world of sin, of righteousness, and of judgment." It was the Spirit of God that made Felix tremble when Paul was preaching to him. The same power of God today makes men fall prostrate at the altar of prayer.

God bears witness to a man when he is backslidden. The Spirit-filled prophet said to David, "Thou art the man." When a man is justified, God lets him know it by a peace and rest of soul, and the whisper of the Spirit to his heart. And when a man goes across the Jordan into the Canaan of sanctification, the witness comes. "For by one offering he hath perfected forever them that are sanctified, whereof the Holy Ghost beareth witness unto us." Yes, to the believers in the first century, and to believers in the twentieth century, the Holy Spirit bears witness of sanctification, filling the heart with joy unutterable and full of glory. It matters little what men believe or do not believe about the possibility of being sanctified in this life, if one has the abiding witness to the experience in his own heart. This is the privilege of every saint.

IV. God gives the Holy Spirit to believers in Pentecostal power. This blessing came to the one hundred and twenty in the upper chamber. Peter says, the same Spirit was given to Cornelius and his household: "Giving them the Holy Ghost as he did unto us." This Pentecostal baptism with the Spirit is poured out all around us today, and multitudes rejoice in the unspeakable blessing.

Some one asks, Why is this second blessing given? Several answers may be given to this inquiry.

1. The blessing was promised. God said by Joel, "I will pour out my Spirit upon all flesh." Isaiah prophesied, "I will pour my Spirit upon thy seed, and my blessing upon thine offspring." Ezekiel declared, "I will put my Spirit within you." John the Baptist said, "I indeed baptize you with water unto repentance: but he that cometh after me is mightier than I, whose shoes I am not worthy to bear; He shall baptize you with the Holy Ghost and fire." Jesus said just before He ascended, "John indeed baptized with water, but ye shall be baptized with the Holy Ghost not many days hence." God has made all these promises, and He must keep His Word.

2. We need this cleansing baptism because of INBRED SIN. This is called in Scripture "the old man," "the sin that dwelleth in us," "the law of sin and death," "the car-

nal mind." "But," some one asks, "is not this removed in regeneration?" No, indeed! The Bible and all the creeds teach us that this carnality or depravity is left in us after regeneration.

(1) Cumberland Presbyterian, Sec. 57, after mentioning the means of grace, says: "By such means the believer's faith is much increased, *his tendency to sin weakened, the lusts mortified*, and he more and more strengthened in all saving grace, and in the practice of holiness, without which no man shall see the Lord."

It seems, then, that Cumberland Presbyterians have "TENDENCIES TO SIN AND LUSTS" after regeneration. Well, that is just what we are talking about.

(2) Lutheran Church, Augsburg Confession: "Since the fall of Adam, all men are born with a *depraved nature, with sinful propensities...* That the Son of God truly suffered, was crucified, died, and was buried that he might be a sacrifice, not only for original sin, but also for all the actual sins of men... That he also SANCTIFIES THOSE WHO BELIEVE IN HIM BY SENDING INTO THEIR HEARTS THE HOLY SPIRIT."

That is exactly what I am trying to teach in this sermon, that all Lutherans need to be "sanctified by the Holy Spirit," to cleanse them from their "depraved nature and sinful propensities."

(3) The Reformed Church, Art. 4, Sec. 8: "But we acknowledge that this liberty of Spirit in the elect children is not perfect, but is as yet weighed down with manifest infirmity. (Rom.7:14-25 and Gal. 5:17.) And they that believe according to the spirit of their mind *have perpetually a struggle with flesh, that is, with corrupt nature.*" It seems then that members of the Reformed Church, after their regeneration still have to struggle with their "CORRUPT NATURE."

(4) Church of England, Ninth Art.: "And this infection of nature doth remain, yea, in them that are regenerated, whereby the lust of the flesh is not subject to the law of God; and although there is no condemnation for them that believe, yet this lust hath in itself the nature of sin."

My! What an admission! All the members of the great Church of England have in them "an infection of nature, and lust which is of the nature of sin." Well, I am trying to tell them in this sermon how to get rid of it; for they must be cleansed from it to enter Heaven.

(5) Protestant Episcopal Church: "Original sin standeth not in the following of Adam; but in the fault and corruption of the nature of every man that is naturally engendered of the offspring of Adam; and this infection of nature doth remain, yea, in those that are regenerated."

We could have hoped that the Episcopalians would miss it; but, according to their own confession, they have this horrible "infection," too, even after regeneration.

(6) Congregational, Boston Council, Burial Hill, 1865: "We confess the common sinfulness and ruin of our race, and acknowledge that it is only through the work accomplished by the life and expiatory death of Christ that believers in him are justified before God, receive remission of sins, and, through the presence and grace of the Holy Comforter, are delivered *from the power of sin* and perfected in holiness."

That is precisely the aim of this sermon, to induce Congregationalists and all others, who have had remission of sins, to suffer the Comforter to deliver them from the "power of sin and perfect them in holiness." Forty years of intimate acquaintance with members of this denomination convinces me that they sorely need it.

(7) Salvation Army: "We believe that after conversion there remains in the heart *inclinations to evil, or roots of bitterness,* which, unless overpowered by Divine grace, produce actual sin; but that THESE EVIL TENDENCIES CAN BE ENTIRELY TAKEN AWAY BY THE SPIRIT OF GOD."

That is a scholarly statement of the truth, and exactly what the modern Holiness Movement stands for. This is what we are trying to accomplish in the hearts of all believers.

(8) Baptist Church, "Christian Doctrine," by Dr. Pendleton, p. 300: "Regeneration breaks the power of sin, and destroys the love of sin, that whosoever is born of God doth not commit sin in the sense of being the slave thereof; but it does not free the soul from the PRESENCE AND POLLUTION OF SIN. Alas! the regenerated know full well that THERE IS SIN IN THEIR HEARTS."

Ah, me! the Baptists have it, too, in spite of regeneration and a first-class water baptism— "SIN IN THEIR HEARTS." And nothing but the baptism with the Holy Ghost will take it away.

(9) Presbyterian Confession, Chap. 9, Sec. 4: "When God converts a sinner and translates him into a state of grace, he freeth him from his natural bondage under sin; yet by reason of his REMAINING CORRUPTION he doth not perfectly, nor only will that which is good, but DOTH ALSO WILL THAT WHICH IS EVIL."

Wonder of wonders! These good Calvinists, in spite of Divine sovereignty, and unconditional election, and irresistible grace, still have *"remaining corruption,"* and they will sin! But all this must cease before they can see God. When will it cease?

(10) M. E. Church (Wesley): "The generality of those who are justified feel in themselves more or less PRIDE,

ANGER, SELF-WILL, and a HEART BENT TO BACKSLIDING." (Sermon, "Sin in Believers.") "But was he not freed from all sin so that there is no sin in the heart? I cannot say this. I cannot believe it, because Paul says to the contrary... And as this position that there is no SIN in a believer, no BENT TO BACKSLIDING, no carnal mind, is thus contrary to the Word of God, so it is to the experience of his children. THEY FEEL A HEART BENT TO BACKSLIDING, A NATURAL TENDENCY TO EVIL, A PRONENESS TO WANDER FROM GOD. They are sensible of SIN REMAINING IN THE HEART."

Alas! even the *Methodists*, with all their universal atonement and free grace, have this abominable depravity in them, even after a wonderful conversion at the altar. And this is the reason Wesley gives for their awful backsliding. I heard an evangelist say this summer that in one of his late meetings one hundred and twenty-nine members of a Methodist Church sought and obtained restoration from backsliding. Evidently they needed a baptism with the Holy Ghost to take the awful "proneness to wander from God" out of them.

Now listen to the testimony of great religious teachers of world-wide fame.

(a) Dr. Charles Hodge: "According to Scripture and the undeniable evidence of history, regeneration does not remove all sin."

(b) Dr. John Hall, Pastor of Fifth Avenue Presbyterian Church, New York: "No church can be found in a high spiritual condition, if the only definite standard is placed at justification. Usually it is in the experience beyond justification that little progress is made."

The experience beyond justification is sanctification, and there the true progress of the believer is to be found.

(c) Dr. Adam Clarke: "I have been twenty-three years a traveling preacher, and have been acquainted with some thousands of Christians who were in different states of grace, and I never, to my knowledge, met with a single instance where God both justifies and sanctifies at the same time."

This striking passage teaches a distinct second work of grace; and it laughs in the face of this modern Methodist dodge, "I got it all at conversion." This was invented to make people at ease while rejecting sanctification.

(d) Joseph Agar Beet, the first Greek scholar of English Methodism: "It is worthy of notice that in the New Testament WE NEVER READ EXPRESSLY AND UNMISTAKABLY OF SANCTIFICATION AS A GRADUAL PROCESS." That is to say, we never grow into this blessing by gradual development. It is instantaneously RECEIVED through the baptism with the Holy Ghost.

(e) The Elder Dr. Steven Tyng, Episcopal Church, New York. He said to those who were joining his church: "Though truly a child of God, you still carry with you a heart *far from sanctified*. A REMAINING SINFULNESS OF NATURE in its appetites and propensities which demands unceasing vigilance. You cannot afford to relax your vigilance over these outgoings of your own SINFUL HEARTS."

What a declaration! "Children of God," yet "far from sanctified," and still possessing "sinful hearts." Oh, how we all need to be sanctified to be fitted for God and Heaven!

(f) F. W. Robertson, Church of England: "Two sides of our mysterious, two-fold being here; something in us near to Hell; something strangely near to God. In our best estate and in our purest moments there is a SOMETHING OF THE DEVIL IN US, which if it could be known, would make men shrink from us. The germs of the worst crimes are in us all."

This precious man did not know the experience of sanctification. But his awful charge against human nature is literally true of all who are unsanctified. "Something of the devil is in us; the germs of the worst crimes are in us all."

Now, I have given you the testimony of ten leading Protestant denominations, and of six great theologians—all agreeing that regeneration does not do for the heart all that needs to be done. It does not remove "carnality," or "depravity," the "infection of nature," "the proneness to wander from God," "the bent to backsliding," "the remaining corruption of soul." Call it what name these theologians will, there is a dark, troublesome, evil something infesting the soul, which must be taken out by another work of grace before we are prepared for Heaven.

3. We need this Holy Ghost blessing because the truly regenerated heart hungers for it. Christians who are truly living the justified life have longings for more of the good things of God. A Pisgah View of Canaan awakes a desire to breathe its vital air. A cluster from Eshcol makes one want to possess the whole vineyard. A visit with Jesus leads us to pray Him to abide in our hearts. Blessed are they that thus "hunger and thirst after righteousness, for they shall be filled."

4. We need the power for service that comes with this blessing. This was the promise of Jesus: "Ye shall receive power after that the Holy Ghost is come upon you and ye shall be witnesses." Power to witness effectively for God is what the preachers need, and what all private Christians need. The churches are languishing and dying all around us for the want of it. Methodist ministers used to be cyclones of Holy Ghost power, and used to light the land with their revival fires, in those days when they were true to the doctrine and enjoyed the experi-

ence of holiness. But now, when so many are opposing it, two thousand and forty-six Methodist Episcopal Churches did not report one convert for the entire year of 1904. The Methodist ministers were never so well educated as now, and never so barren. The reason is, they are looking to everything else rather than to the Holy Spirit for power.

V. Notice now the conditions of receiving this blessing. Look at the story about Cornelius. He was "a devout man"; he "feared God"; he "gave alms," that is, his property was consecrated; he "prayed to God always"; he "worked righteousness"; he "was accepted of God." He was not a raw heathen, as opposers of the second blessing would have us believe. He had heard the Gospel before (see Acts x.36-37) and accepted it. He had a fine record as a Christian, known on earth and in Heaven. And this is the primary condition of getting the blessing of sanctification. One must have, to start with, a "blood-red, snow-white, sky-blue" case of regeneration. Then let him obey God absolutely, consecrate wholly, and seek with all his heart by prayer and faith for this baptism with the Spirit, and the blessing will surely come.

Many seek, when not justified, the second work of grace, and get blessed. They mistake restoration for sanctification. Afterwards, finding that what they received does not measure up to sanctification, they are sadly disappointed, and say there is nothing in it.

When holiness is preached in a community, the most consistent Christians are the first to feel their need, and go to the altar. The reason is, they are the only ones that are ELIGIBLE to the blessing. They are walking in the light, and only such are prepared to seek sanctification.

VI. Notice what this baptism did for them. My text says, "it purified (cleansed) their hearts." This is a death blow to the suppression theory, which holds that the baptism with the Holy Spirit does not eliminate the carnal mind. All those evils the creeds and theologians complained of—the "carnal mind," the "roots of bitterness," the "sinfulness of nature," the "remaining corruption," the "bent to backsliding," the inclinations to evil," "pride, anger and self-will," and "the germs of crime,"—are cleansed away by the Spirit. Regeneration cleans up the *outward* life: sanctification cleanses the HEART-LIFE. Blessed truth! Precious experience! Wonderful work of grace! It is the richest gift of God to the heart this side of Heaven.

VII. The text declares that this blessing is received "BY FAITH." Many fail here. They seek sanctification by *works*. They spur themselves to perform deeds of mercy, give alms, visit the sick, minister to the poor, preach to the prisoners. But all such doings never brought peace to John Wesley; and never will to anybody else.

Others want to *grow* into it. But the growth theory has no Scripture in its support, and no witnesses. It is not found in the religious biographies. In all the holiness camp-meetings we have attended we never heard one soul testify that he had grown into sanctification. The reason is it is not obtained in that way. Once in our hearing an old lady eighty years of age arose and testified as follows: "I was converted when I was ten years of age. For sixty-nine years I tried to grow into sanctification and never came any nearer to it than when I started. I became weary of seeking it by the growth method, and last year I went to that altar and obtained it BY FAITH in half an hour!"

Sixty-nine years against a half hour! What a contrast in methods. The truth is, the time element cuts no figure in seeking this blessing. It is received INSTANTANEOUSLY BY FAITH.

Others try to *feel* it first before they believe. They want the witness to help the exercise of faith. No, no! It will not answer. Faith is the supreme condition of receiving any blessing from God. The Infinite Sovereign will not reverse the order to please any of us. We seek and consecrate, then believe, then feel the witness and the experience. We are sanctified, as we are justified, "BY FAITH."

VIII. Peter said to the Council in Jerusalem: "We believe that we shall be saved through the grace of the Lord Jesus Christ in like manner as they." In other words, "Cornelius and his people first believed on the Lord Jesus Christ and were accepted of God; *then* they received the baptism with the Holy Ghost. These steps to salvation were taken by the apostolic band; we first believed in Jesus, and afterward we had our Pentecost. This audience in Jerusalem can be saved in the same way, or any audience. This is the way to please God and be prepared for Heaven. Such is the Gospel that Peter preached in Jerusalem, and so he would preach today. Paul declared that "Jesus was made unto us wisdom from God, and justification, and sanctification, and redemption." We obtain all but the last this side of the grave.

In conclusion I observe:

1. The text proves (1) that regeneration is not purity; (2) that purity does not come by growth or development; (3) that there is a second work of grace subsequent to regeneration; (4) that it is obtained by the baptism with the Spirit through faith.

2. Do not say you do not need it. David might have said so once, when he was writing worshipful psalms and prayers for his people. But when he committed adultery and murder, he found out his need of sanctification and cried: "Purge me and I shall be clean, wash me and I shall be whiter than snow."

Peter might have said so once. He did declare that "he was ready to go both to prison and to death with Jesus," and he would not deny him and forsake him, though all other men did. But the inconceivable sin was committed by him with cursing and swearing, before morning. He did not know his own heart.

Henry C. Morrison tells of a Kentucky father who went

to town with his little boy to buy some agricultural implements. Riding out of town the little fellow began to cry because the father had not bought him some toy he had set his heart on. The father reached his big hand around and slapped him. They came home, ate supper, and the little boy and the family went to bed. In the middle of the night, the quick ear of mother heard moans from the little cot. She hastened to her darling little boy and laid her hand on him and found him in a raging fever. The father hurried to the town for the physician. The doctor, examining the boy, found marks on the face and asked the cause. "O," said the father, "I gave him a little slap as we were coming out of town." "Well, I find here a lump on the other side of his head." "Yes." said the father, "as I slapped him he fell over and his head hit a corner of one of the tools." "Well," said the doctor, "I am sorry to tell you; but it brought on concussion of the brain, and the little pet will be dead before morning." And it was so. That kind-hearted but quick-tempered man had killed his boy. What a pity he had not been sanctified just before he was tempted to strike that blow!

A doctor in Montague County, Texas, entertained Bud Robinson through a series of meetings, and worked night after night at the altar. He was an officer of the M. E. Church. All through the ten days, he argued that he did not need sanctification as a perfect work had been done in his heart at conversion.

The last night of the meeting he prayed with seekers until one o'clock in the morning. If any one had then told that doctor that in seven hours he would be a murderer, he would have laughed in his face, or thought him insane. But Bud Robinson left him at six in the morning to take the train. At eight the doctor, riding over his place, met a tenant and discussed a little matter of business with him. He told the tenant that he owed him one dollar and eighty cents. The tenant said it was one dollar and sixty cents. Words passed about the twenty cents, until the tenant called him a liar. The doctor, fresh from working at the altar some hours before, leveled his gun and shot his neighbor dead.

He thought he did not need sanctification! The murderous "Old man" was in him and he knew it not. He is in us all unless we have been and are sanctified by the Holy Ghost. As Robertson said: "Something of the devil" and "the germs of the worst crimes are in us all." It is a perpetual menace to our peace and our salvation. Let all who want clean hearts hasten to the altar.

Sermon IX

THE SECOND BLESSING IN EXPERIENCE, IN THEOLOGY, AND IN THE BIBLE

1 Thess. v.23: "And the God of peace himself sanctify you wholly."

I. Experience.

GEORGE FOX WAS BORN in 1624. He was one of the first of the modern apostles of holiness, and founder of the Society of Friends. Here is his luminous testimony concerning his own inner life. "I knew Jesus, and He was very precious to my soul; but I found something within me that would not keep sweet and patient and kind. I did what I could to keep it down, but it was there. I besought Jesus to do something for me, and when I gave Him my will, He came to my heart and took out all that would not be patient, all that would not be kind, and then He shut the door."

Could a second work of grace be stated more beautifully or definitely?

Dr. A. J. Gordon, of Boston, wrote: "It seems clear that it is still the duty and privilege of believers to receive the Holy Spirit by a conscious, definite act of appropriating faith, just as they received Jesus Christ… It is as *sinners* that we accept Christ for our justification; but it is as *sons* that we accept the Spirit for our sanctification… The Scriptures show that we are required to appropriate the Spirit as sons, in the same way that we appropriated Christ as sinners."

Dr. Gordon did it, and the blessing made him in many respects the most potent Baptist pastor in New England. He wrote his beautiful book, "Ministry of the Spirit," to lead others into the same experience.

Rev. J. O. Peck, D. D., one of the greatest pastors Methodism has produced in America, wrote: "God never left me a single year without a gracious revival, in which many souls were given as the seals of my ministry. Never had my pastorate been more favored with the Divine blessing that at Springfield; but in the summer of 1872 a deep *heart hunger* that I had never known before began be realized. I had not lost spirituality; I longed for, I scarcely knew what. I examined myself and prayed more earnestly, but the hunger of my soul grew more imperious. The result was a consciousness of utter emptiness. Then arose an unutterable longing to be filled. I was prejudiced against the National Camp-meeting Association, but a conviction was borne in on me, that if I would go to that meeting and confess how I was hungering, I would be filled with the Spirit. I went, frankly told my errand, sought the prayers of all, descended to the altar and knelt before the Lord. By simple faith I was enabled to take Christ as my sufficiency, to fill and satisfy my hungry soul. The instant I received Christ as my wisdom, righteousness and sanctification, the stillness and emotionless-ness of absolute quiet permeated my whole being. The tempter suggested, the Spirit is withdrawn. As quick as thought I replied: with or without feeling I here and now take Christ as my all in all. At once came the peace of God that passeth understanding, till I seemed filled with all the fullness of God."

Now here is the testimony of the immortal Quaker, and of a modern Baptist and a Methodist divine (all saints of God) to a second work of grace and a second blessing experience. Similar testimony could be obtained from ten thousand other souls. There is, then, a second blessing or a second work of grace in Christian experience.

II. Now, is there such a blessing taught in theology? Let us see if we can get any witness from the accredited leaders and teachers of any denomination.

The bishops of the M. E. Church South in their address to the General Conference in 1894, said: "The privilege of believers to attain unto a state of entire sanctification, or perfect love, and to abide therein, is a well-known teaching of Methodism. Witnesses to this experience have never been wanting in the Church, though few in comparison with the whole membership. Among them have been men and women of beautiful consistency and seraphic ardor, jewels of the Church. Let the doctrine still be proclaimed and the experience still be testified."

In 1884, the Centennial Conference of American Methodism, which met in Baltimore, re-affirmed the faith of the entire Church in all its separate branches: "We remind you, brethren, that the mission of Methodism is to promote holiness. It is not a sentiment or emotion, but a principle inwrought in the heart, the culmination of God's work in us, followed by a consecrated life. In all the borders of Methodism this doctrine is preached and the experience of sanctification is urged. We beseech you, brethren, stand by your standards on this subject."

Still earlier Bishop Matthew Simpson said: "Sanctification is not regeneration. Methodism differs from Moravianism, in that it does not hold regeneration and entire sanctification to be identical. Sanctification is that act of the Holy Ghost whereby a justified man is made holy." Here, then, is a distinct announcement of sanctification as a second work of grace by the most eloquent bishop the Methodist Church ever produced; made more than thirty years ago.

In 1874 the bishops of the M. E. Church South thus concluded their address to the General Conference: "Extensive revivals of religion have crowned the labor of our preachers, and the life-giving energy of the Gospel in the conversion of sinners and the *sanctification of believers* has seldom been more apparent among us. The boon of Wesleyan Methodism, as we received it from our fathers, has not been forfeited in our hands!"

This was signed by Bishops Paine, Price, Kavanaugh, Wightman, Marvin, Doggett, McTyeire and Keener.

In 1866, in New York City, Dr. John McClintock, President of Drew Theological Seminary, in the closing words of his centenary sermon, said: "Knowing exactly what I say, and taking the full responsibility of it, I repeat, we are the only Church in history, from the apostles' time till now, that has put forth, as the very elemental thought, the great pervading idea of the whole book of God, from the beginning to the end—the holiness of the human soul, heart and will.

It may be called fanaticism, but, dear friends, this is our mission. If we keep to that, the triumphs of the next century will throw those of the past into the shade. There is our mission; there is our glory; there is our power; and there shall be the ground of our triumph! God keep us true!"

Bishop Elijah Hedding, who died in 1852, said in a conference sermon: "It is as important that you (the ministers of the New Jersey Conference) should experience this holy work of sanctification, as it is that the sinners to whom you preach should be converted."

In 1832 the General Conference issued a pastoral address to the Church, in which is the following:

"When we speak of holiness we mean the state in which God is loved with all the heart and served with all the power. This, as Methodists, we have said, is the privilege of the Christian in this life. And we have further said that this privilege may be *instantaneously* received by an act of faith, as is justification."

In 1824 the bishops, in their conference address, said: "If Methodists give up the doctrine of entire sanctification or suffer it to become a dead letter, we are a fallen people. Holiness is the main cord that binds us together; relax this and you loosen the whole system. This will appear more evident if we recall to mind the original design of Methodism. It was to raise up and preserve a holy people. This was the principal object which Mr. Wesley had in view. To this end all the doctrines believed and preached by the Methodists tend."

This remarkable deliverance was signed by Bishop McKendree, Bedding, Soule, George and Roberts.

Bishop Asbury wrote thus from a bed of sickness: "I have found by secret search that I have not preached sanctification as I should have done. If I am restored this shall be my theme, more pointedly than ever, God being my helper."

At another time he wrote: "Bless the Lord, O ye saints! Holiness is the element of my soul. My earnest prayer is that nothing contrary to holiness may live in me." He wrote to a minister: "O purity! O Christian perfection! O sanctification! It is Heaven below to feel all sin removed. Preach it, whether they will hear or forbear. Preach it!"

Dr. Adam Clark was born in 1762; a man of rare scholarship, a delight to John Wesley, and one of the best preachers of the realm. He afterward became a prince among commentators of the Bible. He said: "*If the Methodists give up preaching entire sanctification, they will soon lose their glory.* Let all those who retain the apostolic doctrine—that the blood of Christ cleanseth from all sin in this life—*pray every believer to go on to perfection, and expect to be saved while here below,* unto fullness of the blessing of the Gospel of Christ."

What could be a plainer statement of a second work of grace?

JOHN FLETCHER, pronounced by John Wesley to be the most apostolic man he had ever met, died in 1785. He obtained the blessing of sanctification after conversion, and lost it several times by not confessing it. He finally learned to keep it, and confessed: "I now declare unto you, in the presence of God, the Holy Trinity, that I am now dead indeed unto sin and alive unto God, through Jesus Christ, who is my indwelling holiness, my all in all."

JOHN WESLEY, in 1771, wrote: "Many years since, I saw that without holiness no man shall see the Lord. I began by following after it. Ten years after God gave me a clearer view than I had before how to obtain it; namely, by faith in the Son of God; and immediately I declared to all: We are saved from sin, WE ARE MADE HOLY BY FAITH. This I testified in private, in public, in print, and God confirmed it by a thousand witnesses."

Wesley exhorted his ministers (according to Tyerman, Vol. 2, p. 565) as follows: "As soon as any penitents find peace, exhort them to go on to perfection." "Preach full salvation now receivable by faith." "This is the word which the devil peculiarly hates and stirs up his children against, but it is the word which God will always bless." "Do not neglect to strongly and explicitly urge believers to go on to perfection." "Preach full sanctification, preach it definitely, preach it explicitly, preach it strongly, preach it frequently, preach it constantly, preach it wherever you have an opportunity. Insist on it everywhere. All our preachers should make a point of preaching it constantly, strongly, explicitly. Explicitly assert and prove that it may be received by simple faith. If others grow weary and say little about it, do you supply their lack of service. Speak and spare not. Let not regard for any man induce you to betray the truth of God."

In the Conference of 1765, Mr. Wesley was asked the question: "What was the rise of Methodism?" Ans. "In 1729 my brother Charles and I, reading the Bible, seeing we could not be saved without holiness, followed after it and incited others to do so. In 1737 we saw that *this holiness comes by faith*. In 1738 we saw likewise that MEN ARE JUSTIFIED BEFORE THEY ARE SANCTIFIED; but still holiness was our object, inward and outward holiness: God then thrust us out to raise up a holy people."

But some modern holiness-fighting Methodists tell us that during the latter years of his life, Wesley "quietly let drop all insistence upon instantaneous sanctification." This quotation is from a book whose author is a great denominational leader. It is absolutely untrue, as the following quotations from Wesley will show. Six years before his death (1785) he wrote to Rev. Freeborn Garretson: "It will be well, as soon as any of them find peace with God, to exhort them to go on to perfection. The more explicitly and strongly you press all believers to aspire after entire sanctification as attainable now by simple faith, the more the whole work of God will prosper."

To Rev. John Ogilvie, 1785: "God will prosper you in your labors: especially if you constantly and strongly exhort all believers to expect full sanctification *now* by simple faith."

Sept. 15, 1790, 5 months and 17 days before death, he wrote Robert Carr Brackenburg, Esq.: "I am glad brother D— — has more light with regard to full sanctification. This doctrine is the grand depositum which God has lodged with the people called Methodists; and for the sake of propagating this, he chiefly appears to have raised us up."

Nov. 26, 1790, 3 months and 6 days before his death,

he wrote to Adam Clark: "To retain the grace of God is much more than to gain it. Hardly one in three does this. And this should be strongly and explicitly urged on all who have tasted of perfect love. If we can prove that any one of our local preachers or leaders, either directly or indirectly speaks against it, let him be a local preacher or leader no longer. I doubt whether he should continue in the society; because he that could speak thus in our congregations *cannot be an honest man.*"

Wesley wrote to Rev. John Booth, thirty-one days before his death: "Whenever you have opportunity of speaking to believers, *urge them to go on to perfection.* Spare no pains, and God, even our God, will give you His blessing."

On Feb. 27, 1791, four days before his death, he said: "We must be JUSTIFIED BY FAITH AND THEN GO ON TO FULL SANCTIFICATION."

Wesley's loyalty to Sanctification was his ruling passion in old age and in death.

Now look at the Catechisms and Discipline. The Catechism of the M. E. Church South: Question 60. "What is entire sanctification? Ans. Entire sanctification or Christian perfection, is that state in which, his heart being cleansed from all sin, perfected in all righteousness, and entirely devoted to God, the believer loves God with all his heart, mind and strength, and his neighbor as himself."

Question 61. "Can a believer be entirely sanctified in this life? Ans. The believer can and should be entirely sanctified in this life."

The M. E. Church's larger Catechism has this: Question 294: "What is sanctification? Ans. Sanctification is that act of divine grace whereby we are made holy." Question 295. "Can and ought a child of God to be cleansed from all sin in this life? Ans. Yes; the divine command is, 'Be ye holy, for I am holy,' with the promise that if we confess our sins he will cleanse us from all unrighteousness."

That this second work of grace is the teaching of the Catechism of the M. E. Church, no intelligent and honest Methodist can deny.

And Methodist Hymns teach the same.

"Now, O my Joshua, bring me in!
 Cast out thy foe, the inbred sin.
The carnal mind remove:
 The purchase of thy death divide,
And Oh, with all the sanctified,
 Give me a heart of love."

Here is another hymn:

"Breathe, O breathe Thy loving Spirit
 Into every troubled breast;
Let us all in Thee inherit
 Let us find that *second rest*.
Take away our bent to sinning,
 Alpha and Omega be.
End of faith, as its beginning,
 Set our hearts at liberty."

Here is another that teaches the doctrine of *sanctification* as a second work of grace as plainly as language could do it:

"Speak the *second time* be clean,
 Take away my inbred sin;
Every stumbling-block remove,
 Cast it out by *perfect love*."

In an unabridged Methodist hymnal there are over fifty such hymns.

And what is more, here is the ministerial vow, copied from the M. E. Discipline of the year 1900, Par. 151:

"1. Have you faith in Christ?

"2. Are you going on to perfection?

"3. Do you expect to be made perfect in this life?

"4. Are you earnestly striving after it?"

Every Methodist minister must answer these questions in the affirmative in order to enter the ministry. It is a vow that has irrevocably committed every one of them to advocate sanctification as a second work of grace *subsequent to regeneration*. I once heard the statement made in a public address that a Methodist minister who fights holiness as a second work of grace STANDS PERJURED BEFORE THREE WORLDS.

We have thus far proved that the second blessing of sanctification is a matter of experience; and is taught, at least in Methodist theology. But some of us are not Methodists. We are anxious to know whether the second blessing is taught in the Bible. If so, that settles it. Let us, then, consider:

III. The second blessing in the Scripture. There are about one hundred passages in the New Testament that teach it most distinctly. But we will confine ourselves to Paul's First Epistle to the Thessalonians.

1. Notice what kind of people they were to whom he wrote. That they were noble Christians is clear from the first chapter, for:

(1) They were members of "the church of the Thessalonians in God the Father and in the Lord Jesus Christ." People did not join the church in those days for business or social advancement. It often cost them their lives. The church was not filled with hypocrites or worldlings, but with sincere and devout Christians, and to such the apostle was writing. (Chap. i., vs. 1.)

(2) Paul gave "thanks to God always for them all." He was not thanking God for heathen, but for followers of Jesus. (vs. 2.)

(3) "Remembering without ceasing your work of faith, and labor of love, and patience of hope in our Lord Jesus

Christ. (vs. 3.) They had the three Christian graces—faith, hope and love; and derived them from their union with Christ.

(4) In the fourth verse he called them "brethren beloved." Paul never used that term of any but Christians.

(5) He declares that he knew their "election." (vs. 4.) This he could not have known of sinners.

(6) The next verse declares that the Gospel came to them in "much assurance." They did not have "a guess-so," but a "know-so" salvation. This is more than a good many church members have today.

(7) "They became imitators of the apostle and of Christ." In all my travels over the world I have never met any sinners who picked out the best Christians and Jesus to imitate; so I conclude they were genuine followers of the Lord.

(8) "They were examples to all that believe in Macedonia." (vs. 7) This is no description of unbelievers.

(9) "For from you hath sounded forth the word of the Lord," through all Achaia, and every place. They must have been, then, a most earnest and aggressive body of believers.

(10) They had "joy of the Holy Spirit." (vs. 6.) No sinner ever had that, or ever will.

(11) They had "turned unto God from idols to serve a living and true God." (vs. 9) Oh, what grand churches we should have today, if all the members would abandon their idols—tobacco, lodges, cards, theatres, dancing, avarice, selfishness and unhallowed lusts, and serve the living God with all their heart. But that is the very kind of Christians these Thessalonians were.

(12) "They were waiting for Jesus from heaven." (vs. 10.) No sinners want to see Jesus come; that is the last thing any of them desire.

Such were these Thessalonians to whom Paul wrote. Who will dare to say that, measured by any Gospel stan-

dard, they were not Christians of an exalted type of piety, and a deep experience of grace?
2. Notice now what Paul wrote to them.

(1) In the second chapter and tenth verse he claimed for himself an experience beyond justification: "Ye are witnesses and God also how holily and righteously and unblamably we behaved ourselves toward you that believe." That is Christian perfection.

(2) From the sixth verse to the ninth verse of the third chapter he rejoiceth that the members of that Thessalonian church had not backslidden but were still his joy and comfort. Yet in the tenth verse he declares that he is "praying night and day exceedingly that he may see their face and perfect that which was lacking in their faith." It is not difficult to see to what he was referring. They had exercised faith for justification, but not for sanctification: for, he says in the thirteenth verse. "*To the end* he may establish your hearts unblamable in holiness." In other words, he longed to see them that he might lead them into the experience of sanctification, or holiness.

(3) This is still more apparent from what follows. Only three verses later (chap. iv., vs. 3) he writes: "*For this is the will of God, even your* SANCTIFICATION. That each one of you may know how to possess himself of his own vessel in *sanctification.*" (vs. 4.) "For God called us not for uncleanness, but in sanctification." (vs. 7.)

Notice how this is all connected together as a logical and rhetorical whole. "I desire to see you and perfect your faith, TO THE END ye may be unblamable in holiness: FOR this is the will of God even your sanctification: FOR God hath called us unto sanctification." This is so interlocked and dove-tailed and glued together that it cannot be pulled apart, or wrenched from its meaning.

(4) In the fifth chapter and nineteenth verse we read, "Quench not the Spirit. What has that to do with this

subject? Everything. It is the Spirit who sanctifies, as the Word four times declares. Our hearts are cleansed through the baptism with the Holy Ghost. Therefore he that quenches the Spirit defeats the will of God and prevents his work of grace in the soul.

(5) He says (chap. 5, vs. 22), "Abstain from every form of evil." And what bearing has this upon the subject? Very, very much. Only those get sanctified who abstain from evil and are walking in the light. Start a holiness meeting in any community: it will be the very best Christians who will be the first at the altar to seek holiness. Why? Because they are prayerfully walking with God, and welcome all the light He sends to their hearts. The command is, "Quench not the Spirit and abstain from all evil," and then the prayer. (verse 23.)

(6) "And the God of peace himself sanctify you wholly, and may your spirit and soul and body be preserved entire without blame." How much there is in that wonderful prayer for believers!

(a) You can not get sanctification by your own growth or development or by any human doings or deservings. The "God of peace himself" does the sanctifying, and brings the "peace of God that passeth understanding" to the heart.

(b) The verb "sanctify" is in the aorist tense and signifies an instantaneous, completed action. God sanctifies by one of His own almighty acts in a moment of time.

(c) He does it "completely;" *holoteleis*, as the Greek word is, meaning the whole, to the end of all necessity of our being. The German Bible translates it, "through and through."

(d) The apostle enlarges upon the completeness of it by saying, "May your spirit and soul and body be preserved in this sanctification." The Greek word for "body" means our physical being. The word translated "soul," means the principle of life, and such faculties as we share with lower animals. The word translated "Spirit" means that higher spiritual faculty by which we perceive duty and obligation; by which we know God and our accountability to Him; the faculty which makes us companions and fellows with angels in the spirit-realm. These three compose the whole of our being. From the crown of our head to the sole of our feet there is nothing more of us but our clothes.

So completely may God's grace sanctify and keep us all!

What a wonderful salvation it is! Carnality slain! The old man crucified! His vile affections and lusts all gone! The body having only normal appetites and passions! The soul having clean thoughts and holy desires! The spirit seeing God and rejoicing in His companionship and presence and love. This is salvation; this is life; the foretaste and beginning of life eternal.

Then, following this wonderful prayer, is a promise; (vs. 24) "Faithful is he that calleth you, who also will do it." Calleth to what? In the previous chapter, (4: vs. 7), he has said that God calls us to sanctification. Here he says: "Faithful is he that calleth you, who also will do it." Do what? Why, SANCTIFY US. That is what he is writing about, and exhorting to, and praying for. Nothing can be more evident.

A man said, "It took two to sanctify me." "Who were they?" was asked. "Why, it took me and God." "What did God do?" "He sanctified me." "What did you do?" "I let him." That is the truth.

It is God's will that we be sanctified. He calls us to the experience. He will do it for us if we will let Him. If we will consent to obey God absolutely, to *do* and *say* and *be* what God wants of us; if we will put our all on God's altar, our *good things*, our soul, body and spirit, mind, heart, will, possessions, influence, reputation, time, talents, — all, all to be forever the Lord's; if we will consent to walk with Jesus and bear the reproach of holiness in a godless, Christ-hating world, and look up in faith and prayer that will take no denial and claim the blessing by faith, the Holy Spirit will be poured out. The blessing will come; it will not tarry. The willing God will not disappoint his waiting and expectant child.

We have now found that this second blessing of sanctification is not a theory, but a matter of *experience* and of *theology*, and that it is unmistakably taught in the Scripture.

In conclusion we now turn back to the fourth chapter and eighth verse, and read it in connection with the third and seventh. "This is the will of God even your sanctification: for God hath not called us unto uncleanness but unto sanctification." "Therefore he that rejecteth, rejecteth not man but God, who giveth his Holy Spirit unto you." Rejecteth what? Sanctification, the blessing he is talking about. The man who rejects it does not simply reject a doctrine of St. Paul, or an opinion of John Wesley, or of Finney, or of Carradine or Morrison. You are not rejecting merely a *theory* of your poor preacher. You are not dealing with me or any other man. You are dealing with GOD. You reject God who giveth His Holy Spirit unto you to sanctify you. Do not do it, I pray you. Do not quench that Spirit whose work alone can cleanse your heart and fit you for heaven. The Spirit sanctifies, and without sanctification "no man shall see the Lord." To grieve Him is always perilous; to quench Him and fatally resist him is to consign yourself to the realms of eternal despair.

Sermon X
RESISTING THE HOLY GHOST

Sermon by A. M. Hills, President of Texas Holiness University, delivered at Salvation Park Camp-meeting, Carthage, O., Sunday morning, June 26, 1905.

(Scripture lesson, Acts 7:51, 60.)

THE WORDS OF MY text are found in that 51st verse: "*Ye stiffnecked and uncircumcised in heart and ears, ye do always resist the Holy Ghost: as your fathers did, so do ye.*" This was the climax utterance of a sermon which brought to the preacher a martyr's crown. It was a simple discourse. It was simply a resume of the history of the children of Israel, and while the preacher preached it the Holy Ghost sent it home. (Oh, will Christians pray this morning that the Holy Ghost will send the message home!) He began away back with the story of Abraham called out from Ur of the Chaldees, then came down to Jacob and his children, and he showed that the brothers were moved with envy against Joseph. That was sin against the Holy Ghost. These brothers had not knelt for years at Jacob's family altar and been acquainted with Isaac and the story of Abraham in vain. They knew better.

The spirit of brotherhood taught them that they ought not to treat beautiful, innocent Joseph that way. God spoke to their hearts while they were doing it, but they resisted the Holy Ghost. Then he mentioned Moses, to whom the fathers refused to be obedient, but thrust him from them. They knew better. God was leading Moses and they had every evidence of the fact, but their wicked hearts were unwilling to do the will of God, and they thrust Moses from them and refused to be obedient, in the very spirit of the carnal heart always. It was a sin against the Holy Ghost. Then he says they made a golden calf. Ah, they knew better! They had heard just a few days before, the voice of God thundering from the summits of Sinai amidst smoke and fire, saying, "*Thou shalt have no other gods before me.*" They knew better, but made a golden calf, and in doing it they sinned against the Holy Ghost.

I suppose we have only a little synopsis of his wonderful sermon, but I dare to say the preacher pointed to Isaiah, who was sawn asunder for being true to God and delivering the messages of the Most High. I dare say he mentioned Jeremiah, thrust into a dark dungeon and nearly starved, because he would be the faithful mouthpiece of God Almighty. I dare say he mentioned Zechariah, slain between the porch and the altar because he would be true to God. Coming on down he mentioned Jesus, whom they had taken, he says, and with wicked hands had crucified and slain, and when he got so far along he turned to them and made a personal application. A sermon does not amount to much that has not in it a personal application. Stephen turned to his audience and said in the words of my text, "Ye stiffnecked and uncircumcised in heart and ears, ye do always resist the Holy Ghost: as your fathers did, so do ye." Then it was that they shut their ears and hustled him out of the city and stoned him to death, while his face shone like an angel, and he was looking up into Heaven and seeing the face of his God. Ah, what resistance to the Holy Ghost!

I want to call your attention, in the first place, to the fact that the Holy Ghost comes to us and reveals the truth just as He did to Joseph's brethren; just as He did to the people in Moses' day; just as He did in Isaiah's day; just as He did in Jeremiah's day, in Zechariah's day, in Christ's day, in Paul's day. He is revealing the truth today. That is His mission; that is why Jesus called Him the "Spirit of truth." Why? Because truth is the means which God uses to move human hearts. He does not touch us with physical omnipotence to force us into Heaven. No, sir! He just touches our hearts with the illumination of Divine truth, and leaves us to choose whether we will follow God or not.

Secondly, I want you to notice that sometimes people are "stiffnecked, uncircumcised in heart and in ears." What does that mean? O, this is a double figure. Sometimes when cattle are being driven under the yoke, as I have driven cattle by the month myself in my early life, they stiffen their necks and do not want to do what they are told to do. And then that other expression — "uncircumcised." That had a world of meaning to the Jew. To him it meant to be cut off from the covenant privileges of his nation; to be cut off from the privileges of salvation. When this preacher, Deacon Stephen, looked at these people and said, "Ye stiffnecked and uncircumcised in heart and ears, ye do always resist the Holy Ghost: as your fathers did so do ye," they gnashed their teeth.

When is a person uncircumcised in ears? Why, sir, folks who *do not want to hear the truth of Almighty God.* A world of people go to church and do not want to hear the truth; they are determined they will not hear the truth, and if the preacher is there to preach the truth, they will not be slow in declaring that they have had enough of that preacher and his messages and will have no more of it. When the ten spies came back and brought their report, saying. "Let us go up at once and possess it; for we are well able to overcome it," the people raved and stormed and fumed, and wanted to kill Moses and Joshua and Caleb; they were simply uncircumcised in ears. When the Jews led Jesus to the brow of the hill in Nazareth after He had delivered to them that precious message, and told them that the Spirit of the Lord was upon Him, and that He was anointed to preach the Gospel to the poor, and bring deliverance to the captives and sight to the blind, and to set at liberty those that were bruised, and preach the acceptable year of the Lord; O, it is so strange they did not receive the precious message in the spirit in which it was given! But they stopped their ears and hustled Him out on the brow of the hill to cast Him down headlong. They resisted the Holy Ghost. They were uncircumcised in ears.

When the apostle Paul stood on the stairway of a castle in the city of Jerusalem, and went so far as to say God had called him to preach to the Gentiles, the very fact that the Gospel message was to be offered to the Gentiles so enraged them that they stopped their ears and threw dust in the air, and tore their garments, and would have killed him. They were "uncircumcised in ears." We see lots of that kind of people in our churches. I want to tell you that there are people sitting in the pews of all our big, wealthy churches who have declared in their hearts that they will not hear Gospel messages and no preacher of theirs shall preach them, and if they do preach them there is a storm. Dr. Gunsaulus, of Chicago, said one day, and it went all over the nation, that if the clergy of Chicago should preach the truth one single Sunday, every pulpit in Chicago would be vacant of preachers the next morning. I declare to you if I was a pastor in that city and had the genius and power and eloquence and standing that God Almighty has given that man I would have preached the truth one Sunday anyway, if I had to give up the job the next day. Today the churches are dying for the want of the Gospel, just because rich, worldly, selfish, criminal, sensual church members are daring the preacher to preach the truth; and when a man stands up and preaches the *real Gospel* he does it at the peril of his position, if not his life.

Who are the people who are uncircumcised in heart? I will tell you who they are. They are the *people who have heard the truth and then would not put it in practice.* Then he gets down from the ears to the heart and shows that your heart is just as bad as your ears. Some of you will hear the truth, but if you do not put it in practice you will go storming out with the very spirit of Hell in your souls. You watch this audience this morning. If any folks go out when it gets hot you will know what is the matter. They have heard just a little more than they want to hear. Their hearts and their ears are uncircumcised and they will go storming out with the very spirit of the pit. God help us to understand that He saves men by the truth, and the man who preaches the truth is not to be muzzled. He comes from the secret chamber where he meets Almighty God, and he has a God-given message. Woe be to the man or woman who muzzles the preacher and refuses to let him preach the truth!

Thirdly, let us now specially consider who are the people who resist the Holy Ghost. Let us make this very definite, so we will know what we are talking about. I do not want this audience to say I preached a very eloquent sermon against the people who lived a couple of thousand years ago. I want this to be a *personal* message to each one of you.

In the first place, people resist the Holy Ghost when

they are out of Christ, and the Spirit convicts them of sin, and they *refuse to be converted*. That is the message and mission of the Holy Ghost. Jesus said, "And when He is come He will convince the world of sin, of righteousness and of judgment." Why, when the Apostle Paul, or Saul as he was called, got his conviction on the way to Damascus, and Jesus of Nazareth unmistakably spoke to him, if he had put His message off, he would have sealed his destiny. He had either to go forward and bow to Jesus, or simply be a rejected old Jew, doomed and damned. God is going to speak to some of you this morning, just such a message. Woe be unto you if you resist the Holy Ghost!

There was Felix; Paul reasoned with him one morning of sin, of righteousness and of judgment to come. There stood Drusilla, the accomplice of his crimes, the woman he had stolen from her lawful husband; he did not want to forsake her; he did not want to turn from his avarice and ungodliness; his knees smote together; he trembled, but said to Paul, "Go thy way for this time; when I have a convenient season I will call for thee." The Apostle Paul went back to his quiet room, but the Holy Ghost went with him, and never gave Felix another call. He settled it that day. He resisted, fatally, the Holy Ghost.

Some years ago while holding a revival meeting near Mansfield, this state, at the close of the service a man named Tom Taylor came to me and related the following circumstance as an illustration: "During the war when I was a soldier I came to D——, Ohio, and while there had a tent-mate by the name of Charlie Austin, whom I loved very much. One Friday night we went to a mission chapel in the edge of the city of Cincinnati, and heard the preacher preach a faithful sermon. The Holy Ghost came to Charlie Austin and convicted him of his sins and moved him to give his heart to Jesus. He trembled all over, and was on the verge of yielding. I said, Charlie, this is God's call; this is your time. He thought he would go forward and accept Jesus, then he bethought himself, "Oh, I have bought a ticket for the masquerade ball next Tuesday night, and it is in my pocket. I want to go to that ball first, then I will bow at the altar and give my heart to Jesus." Mr. Taylor said, "Oh, Charlie, don't say that, it might be fatal to your soul." But he answered, "Yes, I will go to the ball; next Tuesday night I will be in a royal banquet." A few moments after they rose up and left the chapel. As they passed out the door it came to with a sharp report, as it closed with a spring. Charlie said, "What's that?" His friend answered, "Oh, nothing but the door coming to;" but turning around to him, Charlie said, "Tom, the bang of that chapel door was the death knell of my soul." "Oh, don't say that, Charlie." "Yes, that was the death knell of my soul; I knew it when I heard it. I want you to write to my mother and tell her I swam through her tears and prayers, and have gone to Hell." Mr. Taylor said, "Oh, don't say that, Charlie; don't say that." But that night Charlie could not sleep, and the next day he was in a raging fever; he could not sleep all day; there was no rest for him. He said, "Tell mother I have gone to Hell." The next morning the chaplain of the regiment came and visited him, but all to no purpose. He was a raving maniac, and at 12 o'clock Tuesday night his soul passed out into eternity to meet his God. The only "royal banquet" he attended on Tuesday night was the banquet of the damned. Oh, how much it means to resist the Holy Ghost! Hear me! Every soul that is ever damned, some time resists the Holy Ghost for the last time, and it is all over. No one but God Almighty knows but some man or some woman, or many of them, are getting their last call by the Holy Ghost this morning. If we knew who it was, we would go down these aisles on our knees, if need be, and weep over you and beg you to give yourselves to God; but God hides it from our eyes. You will think of this sermon, many of you, a million years from this morning in eternity. Mark it!

Second, when people *refuse to give up some evil habit or course of action, or set of opinions when God brings light to the soul,* they resist the Holy Ghost. The opinions we cherish, the views we entertain, the theological ideas that influence our political actions—all these have a world more to do with the Holy Ghost than people dream of. He is abroad in the earth. This is the Holy Ghost day; this is His administration, and He is dealing with human hearts everywhere. You cannot get away from the Third Person of the Trinity if you want to.

President Finney tells us in his autobiography of the marvelous revival of 1857 that swept over the northern part of this country and New England; from Boston to Omaha. It was the most marvelous work of grace that this world, up to that time, had ever seen. Fifty thousand souls were converted each week for ten weeks running. There was no great leader, but it was the work of prayer, and the marvelous and matchless outpouring of the Holy Ghost. He says very gently that another section of the country that was committed to the great national evil was barren. While one section was being swayed and swept by this great movement, another section was utterly left, as though God had said for the time being, "You are joined to your idols; I will leave you alone." We learn from this that we want to be careful what opinions we cherish about national affairs, lest we resist the Holy Ghost. President Finney says in his autobiography, also President Mahan in his, that the great revivals that swept over the land between 1830 and 1840 were pulling along certain lines of theological opinion; and that there was an old school of theology that practically threw on God the responsibility for all the sin, and all the dearth of harvest of souls, and all the wickedness of the world; they limited the atonement to a few of the elect, asserting that all the rest of the human race were created on purpose to be damned. He said the preachers who held to that doctrine did not have any revivals, while the preachers who belonged to the new school that believed in the universal atonement, and the willingness of God to save all who would repent and meet His conditions, had revivals that were sweeping the country like prairie fires, and the Holy Ghost was with them everywhere, and crowned their labors with an abundant harvest and marvelous outpourings of the Spirit of God. We learn from that that God had grown tired of having His name and character defamed by the teaching of such awful theology. He may have blessed such preachers in times past, but it is too late; He will bless them no more. Better be careful what theology you hold. Take the Unitarian or Universalist theology. I challenge any man or woman in this house to tell me of a genuine, soul-saving revival of religion under any of their preachers. They do not have revivals. Their churches are as free from revivals as buried Nineveh. Why? Because they are clinging to *error*, and the truth of God and the Spirit of God will not indorse it. They are bankrupt. God help you to see you cannot question the divinity of Jesus; you cannot play fast and loose with issues of the eternal world, and have the backing of the Spirit of God. It cannot be done.

Finney mentions another thing. He says there was a time when ministers could be utterly indifferent to the temperance question and have the blessing of God with them. They did not have the light and knowledge, and God did not hold them very much responsible, and still He would use and bless their ministry; but he says, "I challenge you to name a preacher now whom God wondrously uses in saving souls who is silent on this question of intemperance." Why, you cannot find one in the country. Sam Jones says: "I have never seen a true, genuine, second blessing, holiness Christian who was not a Prohibitionist from his hat to his heels." It means something to get such statements from such men; it means that men who expect to be soul-winners and mightily owned and used of God must be careful about their political opinions; they must find God's side and get over on it. They have to be where the Spirit of God is. Yes, sir; this is what it means.

And then there are our amusements. Oh, how much they mean! Our customs of living. Do you know that our great fashionable churches are being swept over an awful precipice into an abyss of hopeless worldliness and ruin on this question? That great, Spirit-anointed soul, Katharine [*sic*] Booth, the mother of the Salvation Army, said in her sermon one day, speaking to the women of her congregation, "You may think you must follow the fashions set by the harlots of Paris, and you may think you are the children of God; but you will find that you will *never be the bride of Christ.* You may think you must have wine on the table because it is fashionable, and you may have it; but I challenge you that you shall never have the wine of the Kingdom." Oh, these fashionable amusements! How they are engulfing our churches! So much so that at the last General Conference of the M. E. Church, in Los Angeles, it was believed that over one-third, about three-eighths, of all the church delegates to the Conference actually voted to remove from the church discipline the clause prohibiting worldly amusements. God have mercy! It did not pass, but came so near passing that it plainly showed where the church is drifting. Church members may run after theatres, and ministers may run after plays where they represent a harlot coming up out of Hell, the flames coming up after her, and announcing that there is no room in Hell, making a joke of the whole thing, until God says it is enough, and Hell fire opens up, as it were, and consumes them. You may indulge in these things if you will, but the Spirit of God is not in these things. You may play progressive euchre, and, as Sam Jones says, "progress hellward a mile a minute." You may dance and dance and dance, but the time is coming when you will circle and swing for the last time, and will waltz into Hell. The dance is lecherous in its very nature. "It is essentially unclean," Gail Hamilton said, "and it cannot be washed." Mrs. General Sherman said: "Virtuous women ought to blush at the very mention of the dance." Prof. A. G. Sullivan, an ex-dancing master, says: "Waltzing is the spur to lust." Mr. T. A. Faulkner, a converted dancing master, tells us that 163 out of 200 fallen women in a single city told the city mission worker that they fell through the dance; over 80 per cent. Some of you people train your children to dance, and then expect them to get to Heaven. God have mercy on you. The whole thing is from the bottomless pit.

Third. People resist the Holy Ghost when they *refuse to give up evil associates*. Don't you know that is the way the devil is entrapping thousands of our young converts in all our churches? While boys and girls are sinners they are associating with the unclean, with the children of Hell; they get converted and at once the question arises, "Will you give up your evil associates?" and in all probability it will be fatal to a soul that does not do it. A girl came to the Texas Holiness University, who was converted at home before she came. She leaped up from the altar and poured forth a stream of eloquence upon the people, and the evangelist said, "There is a new preacher." It seemed that her very soul was aglow with the love and power of God; but she came to our school and went to corresponding with the unclean young lepers she used to associate with, and her heart began to go out after them, and before she knew it, almost, she had lost her sanctification. God brought her down on the floor one day, where she lay for an hour, just screaming in agony of soul, and crying to God for mercy. I stooped down, and whispered in her ear, "Mary, will you give up your evil associates?" and just left her. Pretty soon she leaped to her feet with the joy of salvation restored, and again poured out a perfect stream of eloquence, saying, "Girls, you have to give up your evil companions if you keep God with you." Would you believe it? that girl went back and married one of them, and just lost everything.

John Hatfield, the Hoosier evangelist, tells of two young women in his meetings. One of them came to the altar for sanctification. She wept and cried, and for six days and nights she kept coming, but did not get the blessing. Finally she said, "Brother Hatfield, I am engaged to marry a wicked young man; I love him as I love my life." Brother Hatfield said, "Give him up! give him up! give him up! or God will withdraw His Spirit from you." She did give him up, and the Holy Ghost came upon her and made her a flaming evangelist, and she has won hundreds and hundreds of souls to God.

The other girl, a Christian, who had great power in exhortation, and who led the service of song in his meetings and sang the Gospel into hearts with her beautiful solos, came to him one day and said, "Brother Hatfield, I am going to marry an unsaved young man. Mr. Hatfield threw up his hands and said, "Oh, Anna! Anna! Don't you do it; if you do, you will disobey God and grieve His Spirit, and it may be at the risk of your soul's salvation." "O," she said, "I think I can win him over." She went on and married him, and Brother Hatfield says that husband is today a low down, drunken sot, and that girl is living in a domestic Hell, without hope and without God in the world. She said to Mr. Hatfield, "I would like to invite you home to take a meal with me, but I do not dare to ask you; my husband might do violence to you." Think of a sanctified girl going down to such a Hell as that, because she resisted the Holy Ghost! I warn you as a father, as a teacher and instructor, who has the care of young people by the hundred in his hands: I tell you before God, when you want *Jesus*, you cannot take some miserable, Christless leper along with you.

A girl went to the altar and got sanctified, and went out in the audience filled with Holy Ghost power, the radiance of it shining in her face. She led some others to the altar, and then went out and backslid in an hour. How do you suppose she did it? After the meeting was over she locked arms with a son of Belial, and when they got outside of the church he began to sneer, and said, "You made a pretty gump of yourself, didn't you." She wilted, and the Spirit of God left her. I ask of you, *what right had a girl who had become the bride of Christ to go out of the room arm in arm with an emissary of Hell*? I tell you young people, if you do not give up your evil, worldly companions you will lose your religion and lose your souls as sure as God lives.

This has a bearing on lodges. I want you lodge men to hear, now. I want to tell you that some lodges have oaths that are a disgrace to cannibal heathen, for the immorality that is in them. Some of the lodges Christians cannot remain in and have any sort of relation to the Holy Ghost. You lodge men would better read over on your knees the oaths that you took, and think of the men with whom you associate. My God, what oaths! Blasphemous oaths that commit you to shield criminals and be partakers in crime. Just now the whole labor world is trying to combine in these labor unions. They just had a labor strike in Chicago which only represented one union, and *sixteen* men were killed in that strike, and hundreds have received injuries from which they will never recover. Oh, the sin, and the crime, and the hate, and the revenge, and the lust, and the wickedness that was represented by that strike and that union! You rage at these great trusts that are trying to take the people by the throat and make every man in his poverty pay tribute to their avarice, but I want to tell you that the underlying spirit of these labor unions is precisely the same, and is born of avarice and has the spirit and passions of Hell. No man can be a full, fair representative of Christ and His salvation and yoke himself in these awful institutions. (Now is the time to go out if anybody is hurt. God help you.)

Well, fourthly, when *people refuse to walk in the light and follow the calling God asks of them*, they resist the Holy Ghost. What do you suppose God calls you into His kingdom for? Do you think He calls you into His Kingdom to sit down in a palace car with a through ticket in your pocket, to be petted and fanned and coddled by Pullman car service while you ride home to glory? Is *that* your idea? I want to tell you that God calls men and women into His Kingdom to make them *soldiers*. He wants them to take their weapons and fight; to go out and make conquests for God that will astonish Heaven and Earth and Hell. There is a mighty conflict between the powers of light and the powers of darkness, between Heaven and Hell; and when God anoints a soul with the Holy Ghost He does it for a purpose. When a great lieutenant general like General Grant is in command of an army he knows just where to place his men. He says, "Sheridan is for such a place; Sherman, you are just the fellow for that place; Thomas, that is your place, you are just the man for the place, I can trust you there; Hancock, yonder is your field," and so on and on, all over the nation. I want to tell you that the great Commander-in-Chief of the forces of light, Jesus Christ, knows where to place His servants, and He says to the Holy Ghost, "Speak to that girl and tell her I want her in India; speak to that other girl over there and tell her I want her in Africa; speak to that young man over yonder and tell him I want him in Japan; tell that person I want him in God's Bible School,

Cincinnati." Oh, God is on the fields! He knows just what He wants and just where He wants His workmen. Woe be unto us if we say we won't go where God wants us. We sing,

"I'll go where you want me to go, dear Lord
Over mountain or plain or sea;
I'll say what you want me to say, dear Lord,
I'll be what you want me to be."

It sounds good in poetry and song, but the people who practice it are too few.

I was preaching in Finney's old church at Oberlin, Ohio, one morning, and after I preached about the Holy Ghost, Father Wright came to me and said, "I want to give you an illustration." He was then a feeble old man between 70 and 80 years of age. He said, "When I was a young man in Medina, O., there was a certain young man there by the name of McClure, a Christian, very active, as bright and talented as any of the early lights of Oberlin. He taught school and was always successful; was a member of the church and taught in the Sabbath school, and was always loved by the people. His friends urged him to go to Oberlin College and prepare himself for the ministry. Then the thought came to his mind, 'If I go to Oberlin I will never be anything but Rev. Sam McClure; but if I study law, I may become "Judge," a great politician and a wealthy man.' He would study on it for a while, and then go back to his law books. Finally one night he went into his office, picked up his law books before him, sat down in a chair, leaning his face in his hands, and meditated and meditated until the city clock struck twelve. He then rose up, and lifted a law book over his head, slammed it down and said, 'I will have my law, come Heaven or Hell.' He had not more than spoken the words until he felt a cold chill run down his back and go all over him, and he felt what he had done. He went to the church officers and said, 'Take my name off the church record. My soul is utterly hardened and steeled against God. If I should see as many people as could kneel between here and Cleveland (a distance of forty-two miles) kneeling and begging me to pray for them, my heart would be utterly unmoved.' Oh, the man had settled it! He had settled it! He had settled it! He lived to become a judge, 'Honorable Judge McClure'; he lived to amass two hundred thousand dollars; he also became profane and drunken, and one day as he was sitting in his soft-cushioned carriage, which was drawn up to his residence to take him to an afternoon entertainment, an arrow from God Almighty struck his heart, and he died in an instant. He lost his soul for $200,000." Who knows but what God wanted him to be some mighty President Finney, and like a flaming angel to herald the Gospel until hundreds and thousands should turn to righteousness, and receive a crown of fadeless glory, and shine as the stars forever and ever?

There are multitudes of people today who are resisting the Holy Ghost in not obeying God's call. God Almighty help you! Why, sir, when God said to Paul, "I want you to be a missionary to the Gentiles," if Paul had drawn back at that moment, we would never have heard of him, or just heard of him as the wicked wretch that held the garments while Deacon Stephen was stoned. That is all we would ever have heard of that man who stands away up above every other character in the roll of the centuries; but he let God have His way with Him. Will *you*? God Almighty help you! God has His place for every one of us. Woe unto us if we miss the place!

Fifth. People resist the Holy Ghost by *refusing sanctification* when they are called to it. Jesus baptizes people with the Holy Ghost that they may have purity of heart and power to do the will of God. The greatest work God does for souls this side of Heaven is to take carnality out of them and fill them with the Holy Ghost, and let them loose on this wicked world to move things for God. God is knocking at hearts. Multitudes of people are coming to the place where they will have to accept the priceless blessing that will fit them for service, or resist the Holy Ghost. Oh, how hard He works to get us; to give us something worth a million worlds! How we hang back and refuse to accept this blessed, blood-bought gift of God! You are *called* to it. God urges you to it. There are sixteen commands in the New Testament, and eighteen prayers that you may have it. Fourteen passages in the New Testament tell you *how* you may get it. There are a hundred passages in the New Testament that point out unmistakably the second work of grace. God urges and prays and promises and commands and entreats, and does everything to get us to seek and obtain the blessing. God in this day is flooding all the churches in this whole country with light. Don't say you do not know what we are talking about. You *do* know that we are talking about the second work of grace, the baptism with the Holy Ghost that takes the carnal nature out of the heart and sets you free and untrammeled. Ah, this is the greatest blessing that was ever offered to this world. God calls you to it and wants you to have it. I declare to you the Christian who hears that call and then refuses grieves the Holy Ghost; he resists Him, and if he keeps on, he will do it fatally.

There is a city in Texas that has, or did have some years ago, an illustration of this truth. There was a preacher there who was once a mighty power in the hands of the Holy Ghost. He had a revival at one time in which more than five hundred souls were converted. God was wonderfully using him. But there came a day, as there comes to all of God's real, true children, when this blessing was brought to his attention; but he had church honors in view; he had ambitions and position and salary in his mind, and he weighed the Blessing against these pebbles of the earth, and finally he concluded he could not pay the price, went back on it, and God left him. I heard a man say he did not believe that man had had a convert in five years. I heard a man say, "I believe his influence in this city is worse than that of any saloon. He is steeped in tobacco and worldliness, still running after riches, going to the devil, and yet filling one of the leading pulpits of the city. One day his cousin was talking with him, and in the course of the conversation in order to fix a date he said. "Yes, I remember the occasion. It was just so many years ago; it was the year I was sanctified." The preacher turned pale with rage and said, 'I wish you would never speak that word again in my presence. I *hate* the very word.'" What chance has a man of getting into Heaven who hates the word "sanctify," that Jesus used in His intercessory prayer? What do you think about it? Oh, sir, the man is bankrupt for time and eternity. It is an awful thing to turn your back on this great blessing.

I was holding revival services down in Texas six years ago this summer, and God wonderfully poured out His Spirit, until men were actually knocked from their seats and fell to the floor as if some giant hand had struck them. It was the power of the Holy Ghost; a marvelous meeting. A Baptist minister's brother who was present said no man living could look on that scene and not see God in it. But that Baptist minister, whose church was only fifteen rods from where our tent was pitched, stayed away from the meeting just as soon as there were seekers and inquirers from among his church members, and talked and sneered at that work of the Holy Ghost. That Baptist minister died, raving in his sickness and cursing God to His face. So you tell me he did not resist the Holy Ghost? The minister who does these things does it at his eternal peril, and if he does not stop it, he will land in Hell. It is the most precious work God does, the work of sanctifying the soul; and whether you are a preacher or layman, if you lift your voice or your pen against such a work of grace, God help you; you resist the Holy Ghost.

Sixth, and lastly. We resist the Holy Ghost by *making fun of holiness, and insulting the Holy Ghost.* A boy went to a holiness meeting in Indiana some years ago and was deeply impressed by the Spirit of God, so that he went home and said to his mother, "I tell you, mother, there is no use talking, the Spirit of God is there. Some wicked young men I know so well went to the altar and turned from their sins and were converted. I tell you, mother, God is there." That mother had enough carnality in her heart to hate holiness. She turned on that boy and began making fun of him and guying [*sic*] him because he went to the meeting, and kept it up so persistently that he yielded and let the meeting pass by without seeking the Lord. In two weeks that precious boy was taken sick. The doctor was hastily summoned, and when he came the mother happened to be out. He examined the boy, threw up his hands and said, "My boy, you are awfully sick; you have only a short time to live." He said, "Is that so? Then call mother." The mother came into the room and met the eyes of her boy blazing with the hate of Hell, as he said, "Mother, I have sent for you to curse you to your face, and I will curse you in Hell forever, for when I wanted to go to the meeting and give my heart to God, you laughed me out of it, and now I have got to die, and I have got to go to Hell." Oh, it is an *awful* thing to resist the Holy Ghost.

Dr. Powers, a noble evangelist of Lincoln, Nebraska, told this in my presence. He said, "My father was an infidel. He wrote a great book on infidelity which never was published. My mother's brother's son imbibed the infidelity of my father, and he became, at the age of twenty-seven, a perfect demon, an infidel of the rankest kind. He used to laugh at me and my brother because we served the Lord. One day in the harvest field, to show his great atheistic daring, he dropped his cradle and rolled up his sleeves and challenged God. He said, 'I *dare* God the Father to come down and fight with me; I *dare* God the Son to come down and fight with me.' God the Father and God the Son took the insult; but the next day, with that awful daring, he laid down his cradle again, struck up his sleeves and said, 'I *dare* the Holy Ghost to come down and fight with me.' Quicker than a flash the fellow dropped, paralyzed from his arms down. They carried him to the house and sent hastily for two doctors, who came and examined him and declared they did not know what was the matter with him; they had never seen anything like it. In the early part of his sickness he began to groan, 'O eternity, eternity; how shall I spend eternity!' He had beautiful, long, curly hair, and for four days he pulled at it until he had pulled it all out. On the ninth day, just as the sun was going down, he groaned out, 'O eternity, eternity; how can I endure eternity?' and he was gone." I want to tell you, my dear friends, you would better play with forked lightning bolts than to insult or resist the Holy Ghost. Oh, the Spirit of God is speaking to some of you people this morning and telling you something. You would better sport with God's thunderbolts than with the Holy Ghost. What are you going to do about this message? Are you going to resist the Holy Ghost, or not?

Bishop Pierce, one of our most eloquent Southern Bishops, tells us that he was asked to preach one Sunday morning at a camp-meeting like this. There was in attendance a courtly Southern gentleman of the old style, who always went to camp-meeting out of respect for his wife's piety, and as the Bishop stood up to preach, this gentleman sat down in a seat before him. God spoke to Bishop Pierce and said, "This is the last message that old sinner is ever going to get; do your best." God's Spirit came upon him and limbered his tongue, and gave him the fullest possible use of every faculty of his being, and he preached the Gospel in the power of the Holy Ghost, and from start to finish God sent it like barbed arrows to that man's heart. He writhed as if he was sitting on a burning chair, his face turning as pale as if he was in a coffin; then the blood would rush to his face again. He went through the sermon, and when it was over, took that chair and went to his tent, and pulling down the curtains, threw himself on the floor. The good, Christian wife watched it all, went to the tent and knocked. He did not open it, and she heard a groan. She peeked through a little crack by the side of the curtain and saw him on his face in the straw. She said, "Thank God, he is convicted at last." Dinner time came and she knocked again; no answer but a groan. She watched the door until supper time, then tapped again, but received no answer but a groan. She watched the tent until eleven o'clock at night, and went again and tapped on the door; no answer but a groan. She spent that night in another tent. In the morning she received the same response as before. She wept praying and watching until one o'clock on Monday, when the door opened, and she rushed forward on the wings of love, hoping to meet a Christian husband; but when she got to him there was an awful look of horror upon his face. He had had a terrible siege. He had fought the Holy Ghost and driven Him away at last; but it took him just twenty-five hours to do it. But it may be that some of you in the next twenty-five minutes will fight the Holy Ghost and resist Him for ever and be a damned soul.

During the war there was a soldier who had one of his lower limbs shot off by a cannon ball close up to his body. He was taken into the hospital and cared for and dressed tenderly. One day the limb began to bleed profusely. The nurse stepped right up and put his thumb over the spot and sent for the surgeon, who came and examined him very carefully and said, "My dear fellow, it is a vein, and the artery is close by; if it should bleed from the artery instead of the vein, you could not be saved. You would die in three minutes." They partially succeeded in stopping it, but it broke out again. The nurse again put his thumb over the place and sent for the surgeon, who when he came said, "My dear fellow, I am sorry to tell you it is the artery this time; now get ready to die, for if he should take his thumb off you would die in three minutes; send your messages to your friends." The man wrote to his far-away wife and attended to some business matters. Finally the dear fellow said, "Now, kind nurse, I am ready to die; take your thumb off." How could he do it? It would mean instant death; but he could not always stand there with his thumb on the artery; so he turned away, and took his thumb off, and the hero was gone.

O sinner, I have been pleading today for an hour and a quarter for your soul. Your destiny is at stake; your *eternal destiny* is at stake. How can I cease pleading? I want to know how many in this audience are going to decide to be led by the Holy Ghost. Oh, recording angel, stay thy hand while these people decide! I want every one of you who decides to be led by the Holy Ghost, to do what He bids you to do, to make your way to Heaven, to conquer in the name of Jesus, to stand up; everybody who is a Christian, and every one who will decide to be led by the Holy Ghost. Now, those who want to be saved or sanctified, come to the altar.